THE MAKING OF THE 1944 EDUCATION ACT

Also available in the Cassell Education series:

P. Ainley: *Class and Skill: Changing Divisions of Knowledge and Labour*

G. Allen and I. Martin: *Education and Community: The Politics of Practice*

M. Barber: *Education in the Capital*

L. Bash and D. Coulby: *The Education Reform Act: Competition and Control*

D. Coulby and L. Bash: *Contradiction and Conflict in Education: The 1988 Act in Action*

D. Coulby and S. Ward: *The Primary Core National Curriculum: Policy into Practice*

S. Ranson: *Towards the Learning Society*

M. Williams, R. Daugherty and F. Banks (eds): *Continuing the Education Debate*

Selected titles from other Cassell series:

M. Barber: *Education and the Teacher Unions*

P. Fisher: *Education 2000*

R. Pring: *The New Curriculum* (2nd edition)

H. Radnor: *Across the Curriculum*

J. Sayer: *Education for All?* (2nd edition)

J. Sayer: *The Future Governance of Education*

J. Tomlinson: *The Control of Education*

The Making of the 1944 Education Act

Michael Barber

CASSELL

Cassell
Villiers House
41/47 Strand
London WC2N 5JE

387 Park Avenue South
New York
NY 10016-8810

First published 1994

British Library Cataloguing-in-Publication Data
A catalogue record for this book is available from the British Library.

ISBN 0-304-32659-3 (hardback)
0-304-32661-5 (paperback)

Typeset by Colset Private Limited, Singapore
Printed and bound in Great Britain by
Biddles Ltd, Guildford and King's Lynn

Contents

	Preface	ix
1	Ferment	1
2	The Board of Education	12
3	Butler	31
4	Parliament	57
5	After	107
	Bibliography	123
	Index	125

To my parents

Preface

The fiftieth anniversary of a piece of legislation as important as the 1944 Education Act deserves to be recognized. That Act provided the framework for the post-war education service, which indeed remained intact for almost fifty years. Then the legislative whirlwind of 1988 to 1993 blew its authority away. Only fragments of the 1944 Education Act remain now.

The purpose of this book is to recognize, fifty years on, the contribution of those who made the 1944 Act, to re-tell a good story, and to analyse once again some of the issues of that time.

As its title suggests, the book concentrates on the making of the Act – the administrators in the Board of Education who laid its foundations, the campaigners who built up the political head of steam, the politicians who built consensus round specific proposals, and the MPs who debated and refined them. It provides for the most comprehensive study of the magnificent Parliamentary debates themselves. I have not written a history of education in the war. Nor have I attempted to study in depth either the origins of all the ideas in the Act or its long-term influence, though the final chapter is an attempt to evaluate its importance.

It is always dangerous to attempt to learn lessons from history (though it is less dangerous than not doing so), but the more I researched the 1944 Act, the more I found myself drawing conclusions. It seems to me now a statement of fact that those responsible for education in the early 1940s did things well. I do not want to hanker after the policies of a bygone era, nor necessarily to defend the contents of the 1944 Act, though it had admirable aspects. I do believe, however, that the historical record shows that the policy process between 1941 and 1944 was, on the whole, excellent. The attempt to reach broad consensus made sense for policy in education in which progress inevitably takes time. The careful preparation and development of proposals, and of the legislation itself, undoubtedly contributed to the coherence and longevity of the Act. The ability of R.A. Butler to combine a concern for the long term, indeed a vision of the future, with the immediate political imperatives was also remarkable. Finally, perhaps because the war against Fascism was being waged, administrators, legislators and campaigners all demonstrated a reverence for democracy which inspires, even at this distance in time.

The narrative of the story is based on both primary and secondary sources. Of the latter, the most important were Peter Gosden's book, *Education in the Second World War*, and Brian Simon's *Education and the Social Order*. I owe both of these outstanding historians a huge debt. The chief primary sources were the *Times Educational Supplement, Education* magazine, NUT records, the Chuter Ede Diary and Hansard itself. Where I have quoted Hansard – something I have done often later in the narrative – rather than give a column number every time, which would lead to endless fussy brackets, I have simply ensured that in every case the date is clear. For anyone wanting to look up the quotations, the task would only take a minute or two.

A large number of people deserve my gratitude. It was Alan Evans, my mentor in my first few years at the NUT, who first suggested the 1944 debates were worth reading. His prompting in this respect, as in many others, was the beginning of my inspiration. While I worked at the NUT, Doug McAvoy encouraged me to write about education past and present, even where the views I expressed did not coincide with official NUT policy. I am grateful for his liberal attitude as well as for many sharp insights I derived from discussion with him. Richard Stainton read, and commented helpfully on, drafts of the first three chapters. All my colleagues in the NUT Education and Equal Opportunities Department were a constant source of ideas, support and friendship. Only since I have left do I recognize the vast debt I owe them all. Tanya Kreisky, who word-processed the text and corrected numerous errors, deserves particular mention, as does Janet Friedlander, who provided vital assistance with source material, the bibliography and the index. I am also grateful to my family, who continue to put up with my obsession with education.

I have one prejudice which should be mentioned. I do not believe the education system in this country has been sufficiently successful in the twentieth century. I hope it may be in the twenty-first, but this will occur only if two conditions are met. Firstly, education will need to be given a priority which it has never yet been given by either society or government in this country. Secondly, politicians and policy-makers on all sides in the debate will need to work towards, instead of away from, consensus. A necessary first step to both of these conditions is to gather up the dreams of the educational reformers everywhere.

I should like to start by congratulating the President of the Board of Education on the extremely skilful and diplomatic way in which he has carried out his negotiations and framed this comprehensive measure, which gathers up the dreams of all educational reformists.

Sir Geoffrey Shakespeare,
2nd Reading Debate on the 1944 Education Bill,
House of Commons,
19 January 1944

Chapter 1

Ferment

. . . the demand for speakers seemed insatiable. The audiences at public meetings included many who had never attended such meetings normally.

Ronald Gould, *Chalk Up the Memory*

Education in England and Wales, at the outbreak of war on 3 September 1939, was in desperate need of reform. The law required children from age 5 to 14 to attend school. Slightly under half of all children attended an all-through elementary school for the whole period of compulsory education. Most of the rest attended a 5-11 school and then transferred to a senior elementary school or the senior department of an elementary school for the remaining three years of compulsory education. The children of the middle and upper classes, a small minority of the overall population, had access either to the day grammar schools, for which their parents paid fees, or to the entirely separate private school system. Under this, the normal progression was from preparatory school at 13 to the so-called 'public' schools.

Most of the children in elementary schools were being educated in large classes – fifty was not unusual – and often in inadequate buildings. Although small numbers of elementary school pupils were able to progress, with a scholarship, to the grammar school, most did not. The number of grammar school pupils had increased in the inter-war years from 337,000 in 1921 to 470,000 in 1938, but this was largely a statistical mirage based on the fact that those who did attend tended to stay on longer. In fact, the annual intake had risen only fractionally from 90,000 per annum in 1921 to 98,000 in 1938. Thus, 80 per cent of all children received no further formal education after the age of 14.

Worse still, for those interested in progressive educational change, the inter-war years had been barren and depressing. Though there was no shortage of ideas for change, in practice the major campaigns had been to defend and protect earlier gains from the assaults of the philistines in the Treasury. Progress had been painstakingly slow and incomplete.

The Fisher Education Act of 1918 had promised much, including a school-leaving age of 14 and compulsory part-time further education for all 14- to 18-year-olds. The establishment of the Burnham Committee a year later promised a new era of partnership between teachers, local authorities and government. In fact, any dreams were blown away by the Geddes Committee cuts in 1921. Compulsory part-time education for 14- to 18-year-olds was never implemented. Teachers found themselves accepting a pay cut. Hopes that the Labour government of 1929 might bring about the 'secondary education for all' promised in its landmark document of that name were dashed too. The party did not have the Parliamentary strength to overcome the vested interests of the Church of England and the Roman Catholics. Instead, once the depression of the early 1930s set in, progressive educationalists found themselves once again in retreat. The May Committee of 1931 cut teachers' pay again and reduced the funding to local authorities. The number of scholarship places in grammar schools was also cut. Furthermore, the Hadow Report of 1926, which had recommended that the 11–14 part of elementary schools should be turned into separate senior schools or departments, was implemented at a snail's pace. Even at the outbreak of war, the majority of schools had not undergone Hadow reorganization.

The 1936 Education Act represented the only major step forward of the 1930s, but it too had been emasculated. The churches had successfully resisted any attempts to extend state control over their schools. Meanwhile, the agricultural lobby – so powerful in the Tory party – had seen to it that the raising of the school-leaving age to 15, promised for implementation in 1939, was riddled with exemptions, so that many children would not have benefited. Somehow, the postponement, on the outbreak of war, of the implementation of even this aspect of the 1936 Act was symbolic of twenty years of stagnation. A year earlier the Board of Education had rejected the recommendations of the Spens Report which called for the advancement of secondary education.

Paradoxically, the crisis of war changed everything. The mobilization of society for war broke class barriers and transformed expectations. Partly this was a matter of people of all classes uniting against a common threat, though it was not until the middle of 1940 that the full extent of the Nazi menace became apparent. It was also a matter of the impact of evacuation. During the 1930s, military strategists had come to assume that if another major war broke out, the blanket bombing of cities would be irresistible. The bomber, they believed, would always get through. As a result, the moment war became inevitable in September 1939, plans for the mass evacuation of children from cities were put into operation.

During this first phase of evacuation, over 3 million children and nursing mothers were evacuated to safer rural areas (Lowe, 1992, p. 5). This was an era when, until evacuation, less than half the population left home even for a single night during any given year. The social effects were traumatic, with city children discovering new worlds – a mixture of pain and pleasure – and the receiving areas discovering the extent of deprivation among the children of the urban poor.

The effect of evacuation in terms of opening the eyes of children is best summarized by a beautifully selected quotation from a boy's letter home in Roy Lowe's essay:

> They call this Spring. They have one down here every year.
>
> (Lowe, 1992, p. 6)

The effects of evacuation on the social climate remain the subject of sociological controversy. The best balanced view is probably that of John Macnichol (quoted in Lowe, 1992, p. 8):

> as well as helping to construct an ideological climate favourable to welfare legislation, evacuation also boosted a conservative, behaviourist analysis of poverty that views the root cause of all children's condition as family failure, poor parenting, and general social inadequacy. Evacuation in short marks the conceptual transition from the 'social problem group' of the inter-war years to the 'problem family' of the 1940s and 1950s.

The mixing of social classes in the armed forces, the growing participation of women in the workforce and the existence from mid-1940 on of a coalition government with Labour ministers in senior home front positions, as well as Conservatives, contributed to a shifting social climate. Once the communist Soviet Union became an ally from mid-1941 onwards, bitter class enemies of the 1930s now found that, to a substantial extent, they shared a social and political agenda.

Furthermore, the privations of the present required a justification and a cause more inspiring than victory alone. Within a year of the outbreak of war, many individuals and organizations were beginning to advocate a new vision of society once the war was over. Unlike in 1918, they argued, this time the people would not be betrayed. Additionally, war had revealed disturbing deficiencies in the education system. Of the conscripts aged 16 and 17, virtually a quarter were illiterate. Naturally, organizations associated with the Left played a leading role in such advocacy, but they were by no means alone. The churches, especially the Church of England, the press, including *The Times*, the BBC, the Army Bureau of Current Affairs (ABCA) and many other pillars of the establishment were in the forefront too. Even the officials in the Board of Education had noticed this social sea change by late 1940, as Chapter 2 will demonstrate.

When Maurice Holmes, Permanent Secretary at the Board of Education, and his colleagues set about drafting proposals for reform, they were responding – or getting their retaliation in first – to an agenda which was emerging in a more or less coherent form out in the country. This educational agenda was part of a much wider movement for social reform, involving social security, a health service and improved housing. Not everyone believes this movement was a force for good. Corelli Barnett, for example, opens his scathing attack on the whole movement:

> While in 1940–1 Winston Churchill and the nation at large were fighting for sheer survival . . . members of the British cultural elite had begun to busy themselves with design studies for a 'New Jerusalem' to be built in Britain after the war was won. Selfish greed . . . would give way to Christian community.
>
> (Barnett, 1986, p. 11)

Barnett observes acidly that:

> Ironically this vision emanated from the same kind of people, indeed in some cases the very same people, whose earlier utopian vision of a world saved from conflict through disarmament and the League of Nations had done so much to bring about Britain's desperate plight.
>
> (*ibid.*, p. 11)

Among these 'New Jerusalemers', Barnett identifies not only the Liberal and Labour parties, but also the 'small-l' liberal intelligentsia, the religious with a social mission and the enlightened establishment. Barnett's case is that the misplaced idealism of these reformers failed to identify the underlying weakness of the British industrial machine, promoted reform of the wrong sort and made no attempt to assess realistically how Britain would pay for the reforms they advocated. Whatever the objective force of his case, in the context of the early part of the war, he should have given greater recognition to the subjective need of people to have a cause to fight for and also to the sense of pent-up frustration so many people and organizations felt following the setbacks of the 1930s. It is hardly surprising that leading figures in society saw the need to offer a new vision as part of the process of motivating people to make the many sacrifices required of them by war. Similarly, the fact that reformers whose hopes had been blighted and efforts frustrated during the 1920s and 1930s leapt at the opportunities present during wartime was only to be expected.

A leading example of the movement for a New Jerusalem was William Temple, Archbishop of Canterbury from 1942 to 1944, and an important figure in bringing about the 1944 Education Act. He had the perfect credentials for the enlightened establishment; Rugby School, Queen's College, Oxford, headmaster of Repton and then Bishop of Manchester. He convened a conference at Malvern in 1941 attended by over 400 clergy and 15 bishops. They studied 'how Christian thought can be shaped to play a leading part in the reconstruction after the war' (Temple quoted in Barnett, 1986, p. 16). Later, his Penguin special, *Christianity and the Social Order*, sold almost 140,000 copies.

Temple is but one example. There were many others, not least in the media. It was during this period that J. B. Priestley broadcast his weekly radio programme advocating his moralism 'of a very English kind' (quoted in Barnett, 1986, p. 21). The *Picture Post* popularized hundreds of ideas for change after the war, publishing a 40-page special issue entitled 'A Plan for Britain' as early as 4 January 1941. The higher-brow *Times*, under its progressive editor Robert Barrington-Ward, was also advocating change. In his diary, shortly after the retreat from Dunkirk, Barrington-Ward wrote:

> I wholly agree with [E. H.] Carr: planned consumption, abolition of unemployment and poverty, drastic educational reform, family allowances, economic organization of the Continent, etc. [are needed].
>
> (quoted in Simon, 1991, p. 36)

With Barrington-Ward at the parent paper prepared to back him, Harold Dent, the talented and influential editor of the *Times Educational Supplement (TES)*, was able consistently to advocate major education reform throughout the war years. His leaders display a mastery not only of the ideals, but also of the practical politics of implementation. He called for 'reform based on a new conception of the place, status and function of education in a democratic society'; he also promoted the need for a public campaign, without which, he argued, reactionary social forces, even during wartime, would be able to delay, dilute and undermine any reform programme.

Another leading figure in advocating educational reform was Sir Fred Clarke, Director of the London University Institute of Education during the war years. His example is illuminating. His chief role in the war was the management of the Institute, which had been evacuated to Nottingham. There, according to his biographer, he continued to play a leading part in the lecture programme and devoted a great deal of energy to maintaining the morale of the students. By the end of 1940, most of the men students had gone and the remaining women displayed, like everyone else, anxiety about the general state of affairs and also about their friends and relations in the armed forces. Clarke worked hard to maintain morale and also ensured that firewarden and night-watching duties were shared between staff and students.

Nevertheless, Clarke was often in London on business and his reputation was such that he was fully involved in the ferment of educational debate. He regularly attended the meetings of a private group of leading education thinkers known as 'The Moot'. Here papers were circulated and debated by group members, and some of the ideas developed there emerged later in published writings. Clarke's own short book, *Education and Social Change* (1943), is an example. In this he advocated an end to the traditions which restricted 'elementary education', a three-stage secondary education lasting from the age of 9 to 18 years, and a better-developed provision of adult education. As in his other writings, his argument has a philosophical underpinning. Social cohesion ultimately depends on faith and love, he argued.

Clarke also attended another influential private group, the 'All Souls Group'. This was first convened in the summer of 1941 by the Warden of All Souls, W. G. S. Adams, to discuss the post-war reform of education. Meeting every three or four months, the group brought together many leading educators, including Adams, Basil Blackwell, Kenneth Lindsay, Eric James, H. C. Dent and several influential directors of education, including W. O. Lester-Smith of Manchester and John Newsom of Hertfordshire. The group's invited guests included on one occasion R. A. Butler.

Clarke took his ideas to a wider public not only through *Education and Social Change*, but also in a series of contributions to the *Christian Newsletter* on such themes as 'The Social Function of Secondary Education', 'The Autonomy of the School' and 'The Ends and Means in Educational Reconstruction'.

He commented publicly on the major official reports of wartime. As one of the few official recipients of the Board of Education's 1941 proposals for reform, the Green Book, he responded during the consultation exercise. He condemned the Norwood Committee's view that there were three types of children who neatly matched the three types of secondary school which Norwood's report advocated. He wrote to the *Spectator* in defence of Butler's White Paper in 1943, conferred privately with Butler on at least two occasions and submitted a memorandum to the Board prior to the publication of the Education Bill. Once the Act was passed, he spoke and wrote in favour of it many times. When the Central Advisory Council for England was established following the passage of the Act, Butler asked Sir Fred Clarke to be its first chair. In this the Minister recognized not only Clarke's formidable academic track record and his reputation as an advocate of reform, but also his contribution to the deliberations on the future of teacher training of the McNair Committee, of which Clarke had been a member.

It is not possible to disentangle the individual influence of Sir Fred Clarke or many other such individuals in the events of 1941–44. Nevertheless, this brief examination of his role does reveal the informal anatomy of the process of educational reform. Clarke and others played a critical role not only in their ideas and advocacy, but also in the bridge they provided between ministers and officials on the one hand, and the popular campaign for change on the other.

The campaign on the ground was most powerfully led by the National Union of Teachers, the Trades Union Congress, the Workers' Educational Association (WEA), and the other teacher organizations. A glance through the small news items in the *TES* during 1941–44 reveals a bewildering array of local, regional and national meetings on the subject of reform. Butler and James Chuter Ede, his Labour Parliamentary Secretary, as well as educationalists like Fred Clarke, spent many hours of their lives travelling through the blackout to speak at such meetings. In his autobiography, Sir Ronald Gould, then President of the NUT, recalled the atmosphere of the time:

> The propaganda work in which I was engaged was exacting. . . . Train journeys were often interrupted, there were no dining cars and trains were sometimes unheated. One wintry Sunday, I left home at 7.00 am, drove to Bath to pick up a train to London, where I intended to have lunch and then go by train to Nottingham and by bus to Worksop to address a public meeting. The train to London was delayed. I rushed by taxi to St Pancras, missing the meal. The train to Nottingham was unheated and of course had no restaurant. The bus arrived late at Worksop, the ground was covered with snow and the meeting had already begun. So, stiff with cold and hungry from a fast of more than twelve hours, I addressed the meeting. Bombing, too, interrupted train schedules and on many nights prevented sleep.
>
> (Gould, 1976, p. 99)

The campaign for reform was strengthened by the establishment in 1942 of the Campaign for Educational Advance (CEA). This brought together the NUT, the TUC, the WEA, and the Co-operative Union under one umbrella. R. H. Tawney, the leading socialist and educational thinker, was appointed its first chair. The CEA alone organized over 200 meetings on educational reform in the first year of its existence. And meetings were well attended. As Ronald Gould commented, 'the demand for speakers seemed insatiable. The audiences at public meetings included many who never attended such meetings normally' (Gould, 1976, p. 98).

This collection of organizations not only set up meetings, they also put their ideas into print. A succession of pamphlets advocating reform, responding to government plans and to reports of committees appeared. Many had huge circulation as they fed the insatiable wartime appetite for progressive ideas. If none matched the extraordinary success of the Beveridge Report on social security, which sold 800,000 copies, they nevertheless contributed to maintaining the pressure for change.

It would be laborious to examine each of them in detail, but it is possible to distil from this outpouring of print the common agenda for change.

At the heart of all their demands was secondary education for all, with all secondary schools under the same code of regulations, and all fees abolished. There was also growing support for the idea of multilateral or comprehensive schools. This was evident at both the Labour Party and Communist Party conferences in 1942. The National Association of Labour Teachers in particular advocated general multilateral education for all until 13, with differentiated courses in the same school thereafter. It achieved widespread popular support. According to a Ministry of Information survey in 1942, 72 per cent of respondents backed multilateralism. While the issue of multilateral schools divided the campaigners for advance, almost all were prepared to sink their differences in order to see secondary education of any kind available to all young people. Hence the TUC compromised in traditional fashion, suggesting that 'substantial experiments are needed in multilateral schools', but stopping short of full-scale advocacy.

There was no division among campaigners on the need to raise the school-leaving age immediately to 15, and as soon as possible to 16. The implementation of the 1936 Act with its school-leaving age of 15, with exemptions, would satisfy no one, not even, by 1940, the officials in the Board of Education.

The reform of the dual system was also on every agenda. Under the 1870 Education Act, school boards had been established with responsibility to provide elementary schools where the churches had not already provided them. This was the birth of the Dual System under which the Catholic and Anglican churches on the one hand, and the state on the other, became separate providers of education. The 1902 Education Act saw a development of this system. The school boards – over 2,500 of them – were swept away, and education became the responsibility of 318 multi-purpose local authorities. The churches retained control of their schools, but were relieved of some of the burden of paying for them. Local authorities were to be required to cover deficiencies resulting from wear and tear on the buildings of church schools and to pay teachers' salaries. The state's financial responsibilities were therefore greatly increased, with little corresponding increase in control or influence. Nonconformists were incensed at the extent of state subsidy to the Anglican and Catholic schools, particularly as in many rural areas there was no state-funded alternative to the local Church of England school. Since neither the Catholics nor the Anglicans proved able to cover the capital costs of the upkeep of buildings, still less of reorganization as recommended by Hadow, the 1902 arrangements were, by the late 1930s, an anachronism and a major barrier to the improvement or reform of education.

Generally speaking, Liberals and the Left, spurred on by the Non-conformists, advocated outright abolition of the voluntary (or church) sector. Of course those New Jerusalemers with Anglican or Catholic connections, such as Archbishop William Temple, favoured something different. They acknowledged the problem of church schools but believed it should be solved by increased state funding. Again, however, campaigners were not prepared to let their differences scupper progress. Given the history of the previous fifty years, any proposal that could break the deadlock was welcome. This explains the widespread acclamation for Butler's eventual compromise, even though it fell far short of what the more radical groups had advocated. As Ronald Gould explained the NUT position:

> It was easy to summarize our position as being opposed to all church schools, and that had indeed been our traditional policy. We still thought it the right policy, but *realistically* had to accept that dual control could only be modified.
> (Gould, 1976, p. 99; my emphasis)

The demand for the reform of the public schools was perhaps the most potentially sensitive issue of all. It struck at the heart of the establishment, liberal or otherwise. These schools had, after all, provided education not only for virtually all Conservative MPs, and many in other parties too, but also for almost the entire senior ranks of the Civil Service, including those at the Board of Education. Equally, those with influence right across the great institutions of state were products of the public schools. Their thinking pervaded every aspect of society, not least education policy. Yet the late 1930s had seen the public schools facing considerable financial difficulties. The headmaster of Harrow, Cyril Norwood, had, on the eve of war, advocated state scholarships to fund 10 per cent of places in public schools. This, it was argued, would build bridges or, in a metaphor used at the time, provide stepping-stones between the public school and state system, while simultaneously assisting the public schools in improving their financial circumstances.

It fell far short of what the reform movement wanted. In *Education and Social Change*, Fred Clarke criticized the Spens Report of

1938 for ignoring the public schools altogether and then went on to argue a more fundamental point:

> We can hardly continue to contemplate an England where the mass of the people who are coming on by one educational path are to be governed for the most part by a minority advancing along a quite separate and more favoured path.
>
> (quoted in Simon, 1991, pp. 37–8)

T. C. Worsley linked the failure of the British effort in the first year of the war to the public school system. Education reform to him was an issue of national salvation:

> We are where we are, and shall be where we shall be, owing largely, if not wholly, to the privileged education which the ruling classes have received. . . . The upper classes and the public schools, having failed to create a better world, seem also to have lost the power or the will to save this one.
>
> (quoted *ibid.*, p. 42)

The emotive nature of this argument needs to be understood in the circumstances of 1940; it provides in any case an interesting antidote to the hoary claim about the playing fields of Eton.

All the teacher organizations, as well as each of the CEA's affiliates, favoured the merging of all schools into one system. Even the respectable Association of Directors and Secretaries of Education (in local government) supported this line. The WEA summed it up in a statement typical of the period: 'Democracy must itself take possession of the public schools.'

The importance of this major public movement behind a broadly coherent set of demands should not be underestimated. While the extent of its demands and the timetable it advocated presented Butler with some difficulties, in general it helped him to convince his colleagues of the need to act, and it provided ammunition for him in making the case for Treasury support. Above all, it gave him the strength to knock the heads together of those in the churches who tended to put self-interest before the national interest in educational advance. No doubt too it provided a wave of motivation and enthusiasm among people involved in education which assisted the service through the difficult post-war years.

Chapter 2

The Board of Education

'. . . planning for educational reconstruction provides an admirable
opportunity for re-establishing the position of the Board
[of Education] as the body competent to lead and to
direct the educational system of this country.'

R.S. Wood

THE OFFICE COMMITTEE ON POST-WAR RECONSTRUCTION

If the immediate priority of the Board of Education in the first few
months of war was the organization of evacuation, it was not long
before it found itself under pressure to plan for the future. The outbreak of war had brought to a halt the progress of reform. The raising of the school-leaving age to 15 (with exemptions) under the 1936
Education Act had been due for implementation on 1 September
1939. It was postponed indefinitely. 'Hadow reorganization' of
elementary education, under which schooling for 11- to 14-year-olds
was being established in separate senior schools or departments,
was brought to a halt. Progress towards implementing the Spens
Report's recommendations on the secondary curriculum ceased.
Instead, the Board of Education found itself dealing with the
administration of evacuation, the requisitioning of schools for war
purposes and, once the Blitz began in the autumn of 1940, the
devastation of bomb damage.

For those concerned with progress in publicly provided education – the teachers, the trade unions, the liberals and the Left – the
frustration was immense. The inter-war years had been years of
bitter educational struggle, in which what progress there had been
was painfully slow and often fiercely resisted by those who saw
publicly provided education as a drain on the Treasury. Like a
glacier, which moves slowly at the best of times, freezes solid in the
hard winters but moves more rapidly in the milder ones, educational

progress had at last begun to gather a little pace in the late 1930s. The outbreak of war froze it in its tracks.

At the same time, the necessities of evacuation gave the Board of Education a more interventionist role than it had played in the inter-war years when its chief concern had been controlling public expenditure. In addition, there was the growing clamour in the country, from press and public alike, for educational reform after the war; and there was a growing sense that it was the Board of Education's responsibility to make public its plans for reform.

The officials of the Board of Education, under their Permanent Secretary, Maurice Holmes, were keenly aware of these pressures. By the autumn of 1940, the *Times Educational Supplement* was urging 'that we set to work to realise to the full the potential of freedom possible within a democratic society' (14 September 1940). By January 1941, when little appeared publicly to have happened at the Board, *The Economist* commented acerbically: 'more than the usual platitudes are needed . . . more effort is needed to see that education does not sink into serious decline because of wartime maladministration' (quoted in Gosden, 1976, pp. 264–5).

The recorded comments of Holmes and his colleagues demonstrate the extent to which such criticism stung. Partly it was a matter of professional pride, partly it was fear that they would ultimately lose control and influence if they failed to respond. As R. S. Wood, Deputy Secretary at the Board of Education, put it: 'planning for educational reconstruction provides an admirable opportunity for re-establishing the position of the Board as the body competent to lead and to direct the educational system of this country'. His argument was that the Board of Education in the 1920s had surrendered its influence under presidents such as Lord Eustace Percy, 'whose general policy was to belittle the powers and position of the department'. The ability of civil servants to find opportunities in the policy process to extend their own influence should never be underestimated. Fortunately for Holmes, Wood and their colleagues, in the early 1940s there was growing public demand for them to take a lead.

Maurice Holmes had spent his entire career at the Board of Education, after being educated, typically for a civil servant of his time, at Wellington School and Oxford University. Having spent six years as Deputy Secretary, he had become Permanent Secretary in 1937. He had the qualities of a first-rate civil servant: an excellent administrator, he had a keen sense of the political climate, an ability to build effective working relationships with each new president of the Board, colleagues and various education figures such as Sir Frederick Mander, General Secretary of the NUT, and throughout a sense of caution which erred on the side of conservatism. He could also rapidly separate the wheat from the chaff. In his memoirs, Butler paid tribute: 'I was . . . fortunate to be served by a quite outstanding group of civil servants: the brilliant Maurice Holmes . . . derisive of many of the persons and fatuities that came our way, yet acute in ideals and practice.'

Butler also recognized the crucial contribution of the Deputy, Robert Wood. Like Holmes, he had a typical background: he was educated at City of London School and Cambridge University. Like Holmes too, he had spent a career at the Board of Education, which he joined in 1911, two years later than Holmes. Newly promoted to Deputy Secretary at the outbreak of war, he played perhaps the most prominent part in the early stages of planning educational reconstruction. He wrote the critical office paper for the Committee of Senior Officials on Post-War Reconstruction, entitled *Partnership in Education* (before this phrase had become a cliché). While the bulk of the Board, including its senior staff, was evacuated to Bournemouth at the start of the Blitz, he stayed in London to provide support to the Minister, Herwald Ramsbotham, and to act as the link between minister and department.

Meanwhile, the office committee – meeting at the Branksome Dene Hotel in Bournemouth, and spared to a large extent the privations of the Blitz – argued out the controversies which were to dominate the debates preceding the 1944 Education Act, and which would resonate through the education service as a whole during the ensuing forty years. It is a striking fact that a group of senior civil servants debated vigorously and in great depth, for example, the future pattern of secondary education or the nature of post-war local government at a time before Pearl Harbor, before Stalingrad, when victory was anything but assured. Perhaps they planned thus because of the growing demand for a 'New Jerusalem' after the war; perhaps because it was ingrained in their professional nature as experienced civil servants; or perhaps they thought about victory because defeat was literally unthinkable.

The committee came into being in November 1940, prompted by a note from Holmes to his senior colleagues:

I find that some of my colleagues, besides myself, have been consider-
ing whether we should not, now that we are working without constant
interruptions, be bending our minds to a study of the educational
problems which will arrive when the war is over. It is clear from
references in the Press that other persons and bodies have ideas on
post war educational reconstruction and I think this is a matter in
which the Board should lead rather than follow.

(quoted in Gosden, 1976, p. 238)

The committee worked through memoranda, which were presented,
debated, redrafted and ultimately became chapters of the so-called
Green Book, the real name of which was *Education after the War*
(Board of Education, 1941). Published for limited circulation in the
summer of 1941, this document set out for leaders of the education
world the Board's views on educational reconstruction. One pillar
of the Green Book was the idea of modernizing and revising the pre-
war education policies, whose implementation had been interrupted
by the outbreak of war. The other was the growing recognition of
the Board's officials that the spirit of the times was, as Robert Wood
put it, 'moving us more and more in the direction of Labour's ideas
and ideals'. They could not afford to be over-cautious lest outsiders,
rather than Board of Education officials, 'be asked to design the
"New Jerusalem",' a fate no civil servant could contemplate with
equanimity (Gosden, 1976, p. 248).

THE FUTURE PATTERN OF SECONDARY EDUCATION

By far the most controversial question in the office committee was
the future pattern of secondary education. Wood's paper on '*Partnership in Education*' provided the starting-point. The school-
leaving age should be raised to 15, with no exemptions. Day continuation schools would provide compulsory part-time education
for 15- to 18-year-olds. The old distinction between elementary
education for 5- to 14-year-olds for the working classes and secondary education in the grammar schools for a minority would be
abolished. All would come under one code of regulations. Education from 5 to 11 would become known as primary education.
Secondary education would be provided for all 11- to 15-year-olds
and would include not only those schools previously called secondary, but also the senior elementary schools, central schools, senior
departments of elementary schools, and any of the other motley

crew of post-primary institutions that had developed since the 1902 Education Act.

These proposals raised two distinct but connected issues. Firstly, should the break, or age of transfer, be at 11? Secondly, what should be the nature of secondary education following the break? In particular, were different types of secondary school needed for pupils of different aptitudes, or should all pupils attend a 'multi-lateral' or comprehensive school for some or all of their secondary education?

G. G. Williams, the Permanent Assistant Secretary responsible for secondary education, whose main aim throughout the ensuing debates was the maintenance of grammar schools, argued that Robert Wood had provided insufficient justification for the proposed age of transfer at 11. As a result, the Educational Theory Panel, a committee of experts steeped in research, was asked to examine the question. When it reported some months later, it broadly supported the idea of the break at 11. It also argued firmly that the door to transfer between different types of secondary education should remain open until 13, when pupils themselves were more likely to be able to contribute effectively to the important decisions. From the perspective of the 1990s, the existence of such a panel, especially in wartime, is a startling discovery. In the present era of rapid change and conviction politics, no such panel exists: the fact that in 1941 it hedged its bets perhaps justifies the absence of a successor. On the other hand, it is not hard to find decisions in recent years where better information earlier could have avoided error.

Most of Wood's colleagues supported a break at 11 for administrative or practical reasons. Cleary, responsible at the Board of Education for elementary education, argued that transfer at any other age, such as 13, would cause accommodation problems, particularly in church junior schools. In any case, if compulsory secondary education was to end at 15, transfer at 13 provided far too short a secondary course. The Welsh Department agreed with Cleary. Wales had already settled for 11 after its own debate, and a change would be disruptive. The only strong challenge came from the Board's technical branch, headed by H. B. Wallis, an Oxford graduate who, like Holmes, had joined the Board in 1909 and spent his career there. The existing technical schools recruited pupils at 13. They were resistant to recruiting at an earlier age since before 13 the interests and aptitudes of pupils had not become clear. Furthermore, since their pupils largely progressed to apprenticeships which began at 16, transfer at 13 would provide a sensible three-year course. Wallis refined his argument in face of the concerted opposition of his colleagues. All pupils could, he proposed, transfer to senior schools at 11. Then at 13 some would be creamed off to secondary grammar schools and others to technical schools. This attempt at an ingenious compromise foundered, as education ideas so often do, on a building problem. The existing stock of senior schools was inadequate to accommodate all pupils in the 11–13 age range. Given that after the war as many as 20 per cent of elementary schools would require repairs simply to bring them back to pre-war standards, it would be many years before Wallis's idea could be implemented. This was the pragmatic argument Holmes used to settle the issue before the Green Book was presented to the Minister. In any case, he pointed out, the Consultative Committee in the 1920s and 1930s had studied the question in depth and advocated the break at 11.

This did not settle the more fundamental question of the nature and type of secondary education that should be offered. Secondary education remained at the end of the 1930s the preserve of an elite. Corelli Barnett, in one of many devastating passages in his *tour de force The Audit of War*, makes this abundantly clear.

Only one in five children leaving elementary school at age fourteen in 1937-8 received any kind of further full-time education, while the remainder were pushed off the plank into the job market. Of nearly three million youngsters in England and Wales between the ages of fourteen and eighteen who were therefore receiving no kind of full-time education only one in 25 were even on part-time courses and only one in 123 in voluntary day continuation schools. . . .

The fortunate one in five British children who did go on from elementary school at fourteen . . . were in any case themselves not particularly well-served . . . the secondary-school population aged 14 to 18 equalled less than a tenth of the entire national age group. Of the 80,000 who went to secondary school at fourteen, only 47,000 remained after the age of sixteen and only 19,000 after the age of seventeen. . . . Of the 19,000 pupils who did complete a full secondary education to age 18 in 1937 . . . only 8,000 emerged with the Higher School Certificate . . . and just over half of these got into university: or one in 570 of the total national fourteen-to-eighteen age group.

(Barnett, 1986, pp. 201–2)

If secondary education was to be perceived as covering the education of all pupils from 11 to 15 and beyond, the patchwork of secondary provision would now have to be meshed with existing provision for 11- to 14-year-olds in the senior years of elementary schools. In spite of the growing recognition during the 1920s and 1930s of the need for secondary education for all, the government remarkably had not asked its consultative committee to examine the issue as a whole. Twice it came close. In 1924, it asked the committee, under Hadow, 'To consider and report upon the organisation, objective and curriculum of courses of study suitable for children who will remain in full time attendance at schools, other than secondary schools, up to the age of 15.' In 1936, the committee, by then under Sir William Spens, reported on 'Secondary Education with Special Reference to Grammar Schools and Technical High Schools.' The exclusion of secondary schools from Hadow's instructions is evidence of the elitism which dominated inter-war government thinking, for as the terms of reference went on, the committee was to take account of the probable occupations of the pupils in 'commerce, industry and agriculture' (Board of Education, 1926, p. xvii). The Hadow Committee, to its credit, made proposals which went as far as they could towards proposing coherent arrangements for secondary education, given the restrictive terms of reference.

As Holmes had pointed out, the Hadow Report of 1926 had argued forcefully that the age of transfer should be 11 or 12. In a recommendation, finally taken up in the Green Book of 1941, Hadow also proposed:

> to abolish the word 'elementary', and to alter and extend the word 'secondary' . . . we propose to substitute the word 'primary', but to restrict the use of that term to the period of education which ends at the age of eleven or twelve. To the period which follows upon it we would give the name secondary; and we would make this name embrace all forms of post-primary education.
>
> (Board of Education, 1926, p. xxi)

Given this new use of the word 'secondary', they argued that a new term was needed for the then existing elitist secondary schools: these, they argued, should henceforth 'be called by the name of grammar schools' (p. xxi).

With terminology now clear, it is possible to make sense of the Hadow Report's central (and beautifully written) recommendation:

There is a tide which begins to rise in the veins of youth at the age of eleven or twelve. It is called by the name of adolescence. If that tide can be taken at the flood, and a new voyage begun in the strength and along the flow of its current, we think that it will 'move on to fortune'. We therefore propose that all children should be transferred, at the age of eleven or twelve, from the junior or primary school either to schools of the type which is now called central, or to senior and separate departments of existing elementary schools. Transplanted to new ground . . . we believe that [pupils] will thrive to a new height and attain a sturdier fibre.

(p. xix)

Thus Hadow foreshadowed much of what the Green Book would recommend and provided a strong influence on the thinking of the officials. R. S. Wood's paper (referred to above) clearly drew extensively upon Hadow thinking. Though government had been less than inspired by the 'tide which begins to rise in the veins of youth', the idea of Hadow reorganization had become official policy and, in a desultory sort of way, many elementary schools had seen their 11- to 14-year-olds split off into separate senior schools or senior departments. The snail's pace of change can be seen, however, from the fact that even in 1939, thirteen years after Hadow, the majority of elementary schools remained unreorganized. Many of these were church schools.

Spens, reporting in December 1938, extended the thinking behind Hadow. The most important extensions were Spens's recommendations in Chapter 9 that a common code of regulations should cover all post-primary schools, that fees should be abolished in existing secondary schools, and that the school-leaving age should be raised to 16. Spens did not go on to recommend multilateral or comprehensive secondary education, except as an experimental measure in areas of low population density or on new housing estates. The tripartite model of secondary education – with grammar, technical and modern schools being separate but equal – was recommended. In addition, the validity of mental testing was accepted. The model of secondary education which emerged in the 1950s was thus clearly foreshadowed in Spens. In the light of the debates among Board officials in 1940–41, what is most interesting is that the Board rejected Spens's most important recommendations in January 1939. Holmes advised ministers that a common code of regulations would place a great burden on the Treasury and that the idea of a school-leaving age of 16 should be regarded as 'a pious expression of opinion'. As for the abolition of fees, he recommended simply that 'no action should be taken' (Holmes Memorandum, 14 January 1939, quoted in Simon, 1974, p. 267). The transformation of the climate of opinion brought about by war could not be more clearly illustrated.

No one in the office committee disputed Wood's proposal that there should be universal secondary education to at least 15. There was, however, vigorous debate about his view that this should be provided, as Spens had recommended, in three different types of school: grammar, modern and technical. The most reactionary response to Wood's outline came from G. G. Williams, Principal Assistant Secretary of the secondary (i.e. grammar schools) branch of the Board. Williams had been educated at Westminster and Oxford and taught at two leading public schools; throughout the debate in the office committee, his chief concern was to resist anything that might undermine the prestige or quality of the existing grammar school system. Recognizing the spirit of the times, he accepted that the 'artificial distinctions which gave [grammar schools] an unfair position of privilege' (quoted in Gosden, 1976, p. 255) should be eliminated. Nevertheless, their legitimate prestige, he argued, should not be tampered with. He proposed, therefore, that there should be selection at 11 (with a review at 13), no fees in local education authority (LEA) secondary schools, and that direct-grant schools should admit at least 25 per cent of their pupils from the LEA free of charge. He did not think the time had yet come for all types of secondary school to submit to a single code of regulations. In short, he believed not only that there should be different types of secondary school, but also that they should be differently provided for, with grammar schools retaining their pre-eminence.

William Cleary, Principal Assistant Secretary of the elementary branch, was the most radical. Like most of his colleagues, he was a career Board of Education civil servant with a public school/ Oxbridge background. His perspective was shaped rather by his institutional role, through which he had perceived the stark contrast between the post-primary education provided under the elementary code and the much better resourced fully-fledged secondary sector. He argued forcefully that the Board ought to anticipate 'the social and political tendencies which are to be expected after the war' and advance education 'in the direction of social merging and full equality of opportunity'. Therefore, he argued, 'the obvious and perhaps the only satisfactory solution is the multilateral post-primary school'. Only this could provide a 'truly democratic education' (quoted in Gosden, 1976, p. 256).

He pointed out that through multilateral schools segregation at 11 was avoided. The multilateral schools he envisaged would need to be large and might be on several sites. There would be a major capital cost. His fallback position was similar to the argument Wallis had made for selection at 13. If multilateral schools were not possible, at least all pupils should attend modern schools from 11 to 13, with selection operating only then. R. H. Charles, Chief Inspector for Primary Education, concurred with the Cleary case.

Duckworth, the Senior Chief Inspector, asked for his views by Holmes, demurred. His response was a disarmingly honest statement of the elitist case:

> I confess that I am not much moved by what appears to sacrifice the interest of the few in favour of the many when one result is certain to be that the quality of the persons required to fill posts of great importance and of a highly specialized nature is likely to be degraded.
> (quoted in Gosden, 1976, p. 257)

Cleary's proposals, he said, would threaten standards in grammar schools. In particular, the levels attained by future grammar-school pupils in mathematics, science and languages between 11 and 13 in a multilateral school would be insufficient for them then to move on to the grammar school. In any case, he concluded, segregation at 13 is little different from segregation at 11: it might just as well be done at the earlier age.

Cleary and Charles were unlikely to make much headway against the opposition of the senior Chief Inspector and the cautious scepticism of the Permanent Secretary. They had little or no support from other permanent assistant secretaries either. Wallis, at the technical branch, favoured selection at 13, as we have seen, but saw no benefit in a multilateral approach beyond 13 which would swallow up the small technical sector. Williams, at the secondary branch, continued to argue staunchly for the grammar-school tradition. S. H. Wood, who headed the teacher-training branch, supported Cleary only in so far as he stressed the importance of parity of esteem between the different types of secondary education. Fees and the School Certificate examination gave the secondary sector greater status, he argued. The senior or modern schools, as the

11–14 part of elementary education was known, would have to be raised to a matching status.

It was he who proposed a compromise. Transfer should take place at 11 to either secondary or senior school. At 13, those for whom it was considered suitable would then transfer to technical schools. There should also be wider acceptance of the possibility of transfers between secondary (grammar) and senior (modern) schools at 13. Furthermore, the grammar-school sector should be expanded to take a greater percentage of the age group.

The debate rumbled on into the spring of 1941, but the weight of opinion in the office committee was always against Cleary. To challenge that majority would have required leadership from a politician committed to Cleary's view. In fact, Herwald Ramsbotham, President of the Board until just after the publication of the Green Paper in June 1941, was more sympathetic to the majority view, as indeed was his successor, R. A. Butler. The Green Book's proposals on this critical issue – which has remained controversial ever since – were summarized as follows:

I.   *Primary Education.*
   (a) Nursery Schools, age 2–5, or Nursery Classes, age 3–5.
   (b) Infant Schools, age 5–7+.
   (c) Junior Schools, age 7+ to 11+.
II. *Secondary Education.*
   (a) Secondary Schools, with a leaving age of 15+ (Modern Schools).
   (b) Secondary Schools, with a leaving age of 16–18 (Grammar Schools).
   (c) Secondary Schools, with a leaving age of 15+ or 16, with a Technical or Commercial bias (Technical Schools).
III. *Further Education.*
   (a) Part-time Day Continuation Schools up to 18.
   (b) Full-time education in Technical and Commercial Colleges.
   (c) Part-time Technical and Commercial education, whether in the day or evening.
   (d) Adult education.

(Board of Education, 1941, para. 5)

Three observations are worth making on this vitally important debate. Firstly, the extent of division among the civil servants was substantial. While it has been argued that there was a Board line which was sustained from 1940 through to the eventual Act in 1944, it ought to be recognized that, presumably, individual officials continued to hold differing views after the publication of the Green Book. Had a politician of Butler's capability chosen to challenge the Green Book line, he would have found civil servants able and willing to provide backing. He must, therefore, be credited with having made a decision to support the line that was followed, rather than having simply swallowed it. It is also interesting that the lines held by the different officials generally reflected their responsibilities within the department. Given the extent to which the permanent assistant secretaries defended their own corners, the eventual line in the Green Book must be seen very much as one chosen by Holmes.

The final observation prompted by the controversy within the officials' group is that in spite of the public school and Oxbridge background of all those involved, it is clear that the public debate over the future of secondary education was reflected inside the Board. In the country there was growing agitation for education reform and for secondary education for all, but only a minority of those involved were determined advocates of multilateral schools. Many, even on the Left, were happy to settle for universal secondary education, regardless of the form it should take.

THE DUAL SYSTEM

The question of the future role of the churches in education proved more complex, more sensitive and more fiercely contested than any other in wartime education reform. Negotiations on the issue continued even after Butler had introduced the Bill to the Commons in December 1943. The Board officials were aware of the difficulties ahead right from the outset. They, more than any, were aware of the controversies the issue had generated, not only at the time of the 1902 Act, but as recently as the early 1930s when reform proposals from the Labour government had foundered on precisely this issue.

In the private deliberations of the departmental committee, however, it provoked little disagreement. This was partly because the officials were essentially pragmatic in their views on the churches and unanimous in recognizing the need for reform. As time went on, they became increasingly impatient with the churches, particularly the Roman Catholics, who proved the least amenable to compromise. On 16 September 1943, on the eve of a meeting with university vice-chancellors, James Chuter Ede recorded acidly in his diary,

'S. H. Wood said he didn't know which he hated more – Roman Catholics or Vice-Chancellors' (Ede Diary, 16 September 1943).

Though the officials were united, they were well aware that it would be by far the most intractable issue on the reform agenda. For this reason, Holmes and R. S. Wood gave a good deal of time to it. Holmes started from two assumptions. On the one hand, if equality of opportunity was to be achieved – and this was the stated objective of the whole reform process – then something had to be done about the inadequate, often dilapidated buildings of the church schools. On the other hand, however administratively desirable, abolition of the church or 'non-provided' sector was politically impossible.

The state of the non-provided (i.e. church) schools was a national disgrace. In 1938 there were 10,553 non-provided schools attended by just under 1.4 million pupils. By contrast, in the 10,363 council schools there were 3.15 million pupils. Thus the non-provided sector had half the schools but less than a third of the pupils. Even allowing for the fact that many were in rural areas, their much smaller average size had a cost in terms of economy and efficiency. This was not the most serious problem. The lack of funds available to the managers of church schools combined with the LEAs' lack of power over them meant that many were in a state of serious disrepair. In 1939 the Board's blacklist of schools with defective premises had 753 schools on it, of which 541 (or 72 per cent) were non-provided schools. Moreover, only 28 per cent of non-provided schools were reorganized along Hadow lines by 31 March 1939 compared to 84 per cent of council schools (Board of Education, 1941, paras 122–5).

The civil servants realized that in solving this problem they had to find a means of extending public control over, and channelling further public money into, church schools. The difficulty was finding a mechanism acceptable to the churches, which were jealous of their role and proud of their historic contribution to education. The Church of England and the Roman Catholics wanted maximum state funding with minimum state interference. By contrast, the Nonconformist churches – who had very few schools of their own – resented state money being spent on, as they saw it, the promotion of the Anglican and Catholic religions. It was they who, in 1902, had produced a huge wave of opposition to Balfour's Education Act on the grounds that it provided for, in Lloyd George's phrase, 'Rome on the rates'. This bitter controversy had left a profound impression on a young MP at the time. He was now Prime Minister.

Two anomalies particularly irked the board officials. However much spare capacity an LEA had, it had no power to close any non-provided school with thirty or more pupils unless there was another school of the same denomination available. In addition, the law allowed for a new non-provided school to be established even where LEAs were already able to accommodate adequately all the pupils in the area. The combination of these two factors made it difficult for LEAs to plan sensibly.

Holmes proposed three possible ways of solving these problems. Firstly, the status quo could be continued with the managers of church schools being exhorted to do better. If this failed, as was likely in the case of most schools, Holmes's second option would have given LEAs responsibility for the buildings of church schools and the appointment of their teachers. In addition, they would have the power to close them altogether subject to an appeal from the school's managers to the Board. Denominational education, however, would remain under the managers' control and at their expense.

Under his third option, LEAs would be empowered to make grants of 50-75 per cent towards upkeep of buildings and would appoint most teachers. Denominational education would be provided by 'reserved teachers' appointed by the school's managers.

Wynn Wheldon, the Permanent Secretary for Wales, believed Holmes's proposals might revive the non-provided schools in the principality, where he believed they were in decline. He therefore promoted the additional idea of non-provided schools being transferred voluntarily to LEAs.

Cleary, on this theme, as on others, more radical than his colleagues, favoured outright abolition of the non-provided sector. If this was not possible, he thought Holmes's three options should be given more bite by the addition of a tight time limit to the first issue. In addition, managers of schools would have to choose between the options: if they wanted the first option, the onus of proof would be on them to demonstrate their ability to maintain the school.

In the Green Book, the problems were uncompromisingly set out. The existing arrangements were unsatisfactory. The reforms of secondary education proposed in the Green Book, which had widespread support, would exacerbate a situation in which church schools were required 'to shoulder a financial burden far in excess of their capacity'. Furthermore:

> the need for modernisation or replacement of much of the non-provided school accommodation for junior and infant children, a [large] number of whom are housed in conditions little short of scandalous, faces the churches with a financial problem greater in extent and no less urgent than that in respect of senior children, a problem which they have shown themselves quite unable to meet in recent years.
>
> (Board of Education, 1941, para. 127)

It stopped short of being specific about how to solve the problem. Instead, it proposed in generalized terms the kind of deal Holmes had begun to flesh out:

> public opinion would not tolerate what might mean the large scale abolition of non-provided schools, but would look rather for some measure of extended financial assistance, accompanied, as it must be, by such extended public control as is necessary, not simply to secure a quid pro quo, but to ensure effective and economical organisation and development of both primary and secondary education.
>
> (*ibid*., para. 128)

This was the state of the religious debate when R. A. Butler arrived on the scene as President of the Board of Education in July 1941. It would take many painstaking hours of negotiations with the conflicting parties to move from here to the proposals finally approved in 1944. Given the time dedicated to the issue, it is perhaps most remarkable how little changed over that time; in the end it was a question of refinement rather than rethinking. Butler's skill was overwhelmingly political, rather than educational.

THE FUTURE OF LOCAL GOVERNMENT INVOLVEMENT IN EDUCATION

Given that the overriding goal of the wartime reforms was to introduce secondary education for all, it was inevitable that those local education authorities which had responsibility solely for elementary education would be called into question. These were the so-called Part III authorities. The existing arrangement, like so many other aspects of the British constitution, owed more to messy political compromise than to either administrative convenience or educational advance.

The complex pattern facing board officials in the early 1940s was an inheritance from the Victorian era. Sir John Gorst's abortive 1896 Education Bill had proposed that the administration of all types of education should be the responsibility of the counties and county boroughs. This had provoked a storm of opposition from both the non-county boroughs and the urban districts. As a result, the framers of the 1902 Act proposed two types of local education authority in order to avoid another storm.

There were those with responsibility for both elementary and secondary (or higher as it was then known) education: the county boroughs and counties. There were also those which had responsibility solely for elementary education: non-county boroughs with populations over 10,000 and urban districts with populations over 20,000. This arrangement had increasingly proved to be a barrier to educational progress. The commissions and consultative committees that examined either local government or education in the inter-war years repeatedly pointed to the difficulties. The Board of Education had long been committed to resolving it. As the Permanent Secretary in 1927, Sir Amherst Selby Bigge, argued: 'It is to be hoped that the realisation of the great and increasing inconveniences of the present arrangements will lead, whether by way of central or local action, to a real effort to overcome them.'

The Hadow Report proposed three possible solutions. Local co-operation could be encouraged. The responsibilities of all but the largest Part III authorities could be transferred to Part II authorities. Or the responsibilities of both could be merged in new regional authorities. The Spens Report endorsed this approach, but pointed out that the third option was unlikely to be a serious runner politically.

The chances of serious reform happening spontaneously at local level were negligible given the jealous guarding of powers characteristic of local government. As we watch the unwholesome squabbles between counties and districts that mark the 1990s, this is easy to understand. However, it was only slightly less difficult for central government, particularly Conservative central government, to take on the local vested interests.

The Green Book nevertheless made the case forcefully:

the general arguments in favour of a single type of Local Education Authority are strongly reinforced by the proposals in regard to the layout of the education system . . . If all schools for children over 11 are to be regarded as secondary and dealt with under a single code of regulations, then the field of elementary education will be limited to education for children up to the age of 11. . . . In the words of the Select Committee on Estimates, the suggestion that the functions of Authorities for elementary education should be limited to the education of children up to 11 'is only to be made to be rejected'.

(Board of Education, 1941, para. 118)

Having made the case for change, however, the Green Book ducked out of making firm proposals. 'The precise method of constituting Local Education Authorities, assuming that the principle of a single type of Authority is accepted, is outside the scope of this Memorandum' (*ibid*, para. 119). A move to a single type of LEA would inevitably involve conflict with the influential Association of Education Committees and its formidable Secretary, Sir Percival Sharp. The resolution of the question was another matter left ultimately to R. A. Butler, and his Parliamentary Secretary, James Chuter Ede.

OTHER PROPOSALS IN THE GREEN BOOK

So far, we have looked at the Green Book's proposals on the major issues likely to cause controversy. Its 157 paragraphs contain proposals on a wide range of other themes, many of which were taken up in the 1944 Education Act without generating any great debate. It advocated, for example, reviving the 1918 Education Act's proposals for day continuation schools. Young people who had left school at 15 would be required to attend them for 280 hours per year up to the age of 18. The Green Book's authors hoped that the time would be made up of two half-days of 3.5 hours every week. The failure to implement this proposal, both between the wars and after World War II, is perhaps the biggest single tragedy in the uncomfortable history of twentieth-century education in England and Wales.

An extension of the youth service, 'utilising in full the assistance of the voluntary organisations' (Board of Education, 1941, summary, No. 14) was also proposed. It would be complementary to the work of the day continuation schools, and contribute to the ambitious goal of 'a complete system . . . covering the social, physical and education welfare of adolescents' (*ibid.*) There were further proposals to improve the relationship between education and industry and to bring coherence to the system of grants for students at university. Heightened wartime concern for the health and physical well-being of children is also reflected in the text.

Finally, the Green Book gave attention to the important question of the recruitment and training of teachers. The Board officials of the time recognized that without a sufficient supply of well-prepared teachers, the whole ambitious scheme of reform could prove to be a hollow promise. They proposed therefore that the two-year training college course be extended to three years, of which a large part of the second year would be spent in schools. The four-year university course would be abolished: instead graduates would be offered a year's professional training with appropriate grants. They also recognized the need to improve what they described as the 'spasmodic' provision of in-service education. Later in the war, the immediate problems of shortage and demobilization would come to the fore as indeed they did in both the McNair Report and in the Parliamentary debates in 1944, but at this stage they were not examined.

THE PUBLICATION OF THE GREEN BOOK

On 13 May 1941 the final revised chapters of the Green Book were presented to the President of the Board, Herwald Ramsbotham. He approved them the same day. Given the nature of the Green Book, this did not, and was not intended to, amount to a full political endorsement. On the other hand, it was important that it contained neither proposals with which he violently disagreed nor any hostages to fortune. Holmes's foreword explained:

> The Memorandum must not be taken as embodying the Board's considered conclusions . . . in order, however, to ascertain [the views of various interest groups], there are obvious advantages in putting before those who can speak for them a document which may serve as a basis for discussion.
>
> (Board of Education, 1941, foreword)

The Green Book's proposals had been widely trailed, not least by Ramsbotham himself. At the NUT's Easter conference in Morecambe, he had argued that reform could only take place with the active support of the Board's partners. To this end, he said, consultation to discover the views of the various partners would take place. At a meeting of the NUT in London soon after, he announced that a document for discussion would be available shortly, and went on to describe some of the Green Book's proposals.

In spite of the disclaimers in the foreword and the widespread advance publicity, the Board attempted to limit strictly access to the Green Book when it emerged. It was sent to twenty-nine organizations and individuals, who were asked to respond. Holmes in particular was anxious, in traditional Civil Service fashion, about opening up the debate to 'amateurs' before there was a clear political direction. What resulted, however, was a bungle. The Green Book was neither publicly available nor confidential. W. O. Lester-Smith quipped, in a famous remark, that it was launched 'in a blaze of secrecy'. This about summed it up. Chuter Ede's Parliamentary Private Secretary received a copy only after Ede had made a formal written request to the President of the Board. The General Secretary of the Labour Party, meanwhile, found he had to take it up with Winston Churchill himself before he was given one.

Nevertheless, responses eventually came in. The NUT published a response with a darker green cover. This enabled Ronald Gould, later President and then General Secretary of the Union, to describe the Board's proposals as 'the Light Green Book' as opposed to the NUT's 'Sage Green Book' (Gould, 1976, p. 89). The 'Sage' proposals were characteristic of the more radical agenda of the time: a school-leaving age of 16, universal secondary education, a single code of regulations and an end to the Dual System. This agenda gained, as we have seen, widespread support in the country during the war years, but before any of these proposals came to fruition there had been a shift in the political leadership at the Board of Education. R. A. Butler, who had such a profound influence on the course of educational development over the next four years, had arrived.

Chapter 3

Butler

[Churchill] said that if I wanted to go there he'd be glad to send me
but that he wouldn't like to wipe children's noses and smack their
behinds during the war.

R. A. Butler

THE APPOINTMENT OF R. A. BUTLER

There is a lack of clarity about why Herwald Ramsbotham, then
President of the Board of Education, was replaced in July 1941. It
appears that Ramsbotham's speeches had disturbed Churchill, who
thought the advocacy of educational reform would distract concen-
tration from the war effort, cause controversy and upset the large
number of diehard Conservative MPs on whose support Churchill
and the War Cabinet depended. Kevin Jeffereys (1984) claims that
this was 'the main cause behind Ramsbotham's removal from the
Board'. Ramsbotham himself was reluctant to depart, but the
evidence supports Jeffereys's conclusion. According to Chuter Ede,
Butler was aware of 'whispers of displeasure at Ramsbotham's
advanced ideas' (Ede Diary, 21 July 1941). If so, it was an indica-
tion of the gulf between Conservative backbenchers and opinion
in the country. There Ramsbotham had been criticized for lack
of imagination, even by respectable publications such as *The
Economist*.

There is also doubt about why R. A. Butler was the chosen
successor. Butler himself, at different times later in his life, gave
two contradictory accounts of his appointment. There seems little
doubt, however, that at the time it was not considered, by Churchill
at any rate, to be a promotion for Butler. Nevertheless, Butler
soon realized the opportunity that the appointment provided.
Given his relationship with Churchill over the previous decade,
he could certainly count himself lucky. Indeed, over the preceding

months, he had expected the political equivalent of exile.

Butler had been born into one of the leading Conservative families in the country. Several generations of the Butler clan had been involved in Conservative party politics and in the academic life of Cambridge University. R. A. Butler was simply fulfilling family tradition when he gained a first at Cambridge and became President of the Union before being appointed to a fellowship at Corpus Christi College. He had the good fortune to have been born a year or so too late to serve in World War I. His political career was almost inevitable. While still at Corpus Christi, he became an assistant to Samuel Hoare who was then Secretary of State for Air. Soon after, he married Sidney Courtauld, the daughter of one of the country's leading industrial magnates, Samuel Courtauld. Then, at the age of 26, he was elected in the 1929 general election to represent Saffron Walden, a seat which remained his until he retired from politics in 1964.

The career opportunity provided by his unique combination of family links to politics, academia and (through marriage) industry was greatly enhanced by talent of a high order. He moved into the political fast lane. His uncle, Geoffrey Butler, was at the time MP for Cambridge University and politically associated with the rising stars of the Conservative party, Samuel Hoare, Neville Chamberlain and Edward Wood, Lord Halifax. By 1932, after less than three years in Parliament, R. A. Butler had become a minister at the India Office, under his mentor Samuel Hoare, who was Secretary for India. There, Butler played a leading part in preparing, and piloting through the Commons, the India Bill, which gave a limited degree of self-government to the subcontinent. It was in this role that he first collided with Winston Churchill.

At that time it was generally accepted that Churchill was on his way out of politics. These were his 'wilderness years' after a long and colourful political career which had combined remarkable achievements and cases of severe misjudgement in roughly equal measure. If there was anything which matched Churchill's enthusiasm for war, it was his belief in the benefits of the empire. By the time he had reached his early twenties, he had, after all, fought for the maintenance of the empire in three conflicts as far apart as India, Sudan and South Africa, and he was passionately opposed to the growing consensus that a degree of self-government for India was both good and inevitable. He predicted, in the emotive debate on the

India Bill, that as a result of its proposals, 'India will fall back quite rapidly through the centuries into the barbarism and privations of the Middle Ages'. Churchill, who claimed at the time that but for India he would have left politics altogether, fought Hoare and Butler in the party as well as Parliament. There he found a substantial minority prepared to provide him with passionate support.

As a result, the pressure on the young Butler was intense. His firmness, calmness and his astute mastery of the arguments won him widespread respect, particularly in the upper echelons of the party. Baldwin, the party leader, was impressed. Apart from the personal angle, this episode is important for the experience it gave Butler in managing the Parliamentary process. In 1943–44 he drew on all the skills of negotiation and political tactics he had learnt a decade earlier.

Butler's next ministerial office threw him up against Churchill again. In February 1938 Anthony Eden resigned from the post of Foreign Secretary in protest at the continuation of the policy of appeasement which characterized the British government's response to the growing aggression of Hitler and Mussolini. Lord Cranborne, his deputy, resigned too. Lord Halifax became Foreign Secretary with Butler as his deputy and representative in the House of Commons. Butler became a leading apologist for appeasement, and remained so until the famous debate in April 1940 which brought Churchill to power, at the head of a coalition government, and drove Neville Chamberlain from office.

Churchill had opposed appeasement and called for rearmament since the mid-1930s. The passion that had failed to stop the India Bill was now channelled into alerting the nation to the dangers of Fascism. With Butler representing the Foreign Office in the House of Commons through the Munich crisis and beyond, he became the target of many of Churchill's attacks. When Churchill became Prime Minister, Butler expected to be replaced sooner or later.

Churchill in fact moved with more caution than might have been expected. The appeasers were dispersed from the centres of power over a period of a year or so. Butler was lucky to survive at the Foreign Office, since within a month or so he provided Churchill with a golden opportunity to remove him, had he wished. On 22 June 1940, the day Pétain surrendered to the Germans, Butler met, during the course of his duties, Bjorn Prytz, a Swedish minister. The exact nature of their conversation is unclear. According to one account,

Butler told Prytz that a negotiated end to the war was still possible and that in foreign policy 'common sense not bravado' of the type that could be expected from 'diehards like Churchill' would prevail.

When accounts reached him, Churchill saw this as an act of disloyalty and defeatism. He knew that Halifax had advocated exactly this line in the Cabinet a month or so before, so he took it up with both Halifax and Butler. No doubt Halifax stood up for his protégé and Butler gave a good account of himself. In any event, he survived. Churchill chose instead to issue a note to all departments urging all those 'in high places to set an example of steadfastness and resolution'. Whether Churchill took this course because he had developed a sneaking regard for the talents of his young adversary of the 1930s is not recorded. Over the months that ensued, the high priests of appeasement were shuffled off the scene. In March 1941 Eden returned to the Foreign Office while Halifax became ambassador in Washington. Hoare, Butler's previous mentor, had already become ambassador in Madrid. For Butler, it seemed only a matter of time before he followed them into political exile.

At this time he wrote to Ramsbotham asking for a copy of the Green Book. He claims that he had heard that Ramsbotham was hoping to leave the Board, but there is no other evidence for this. In his letter to Ramsbotham, Butler argued that he wanted to serve a useful purpose as a link between the Central Committee of the party and the government on domestic issues. Certainly Butler had already shown an interest, unusual among leading Conservatives, in post-war reconstruction. Unlike many of his colleagues, he had already realized that the war would transform social aspirations.

Soon after this letter, Butler was summoned to see Churchill, and probably expected the worst. Butler has given two accounts of what happened next, both of which are worth quoting at length.

In a television interview in 1966 (*The Listener*, 28 July), Butler claimed that he took the initiative in suggesting he should take on the presidency of the Board of Education. According to this account, after being offered an unspecified post abroad:

> [I] said my family had always been interested in education and also I had great hopes of making some reform during the war. [Churchill] said that if I wanted to go there he'd be glad to send me, but that he wouldn't like to wipe children's noses and smack their behinds during the war: he did not know what I'd be doing there – so I said I would keep very busy and let him know.

Churchill's comment about the Board of Education in this account rings true. He saw it as a low-status post at the best of times. Early in his political career he had turned down a post at the Local Government Board, saying, characteristically, that he did not want to spend time shut up in a soup kitchen with Beatrice Webb. In mid-1941, when Britain's future hung in the balance and the war absorbed him totally, it must have seemed remarkably unimportant.

In his autobiography, published some five years later than the interview in the *Listener*, Butler's account is rather different. Churchill, he says, told him that it was time he was promoted:

> I now want you to go to the Board of Education. I think you can leave your mark there. You will be independent.

Having suggested to Butler that he would have to administer the difficult process of evacuation, he changed the subject:

> I am too old now to think you can change people's natures. Everyone has to learn to defend himself. I should not object if you could introduce a note of patriotism into the schools.

Recalling a conversation with Butler the previous week, he grinned and said, 'tell the children that Wolfe won Quebec'. Butler commented that though he would like to influence what was taught in schools, this was frowned upon. Churchill turned serious and added, 'Of course not by instruction or order, but by suggestion' (Butler, 1971, p. 90). Butler goes on to suggest that Churchill appeared surprised that he was looking forward to the new post.

Both accounts were given many years after the event; both include typically Churchillian remarks. In any case, there is more consistency than appears at first sight. Clearly Churchill attached little importance to the post. In the Prime Minister's mind, Butler was being moved away from the action, whether or not technically speaking this was promotion. Churchill's obsession with winning the war is powerfully evident in both. Secondly, it is clear that Churchill did not have education reform in mind; his focus was on the contribution the Board of Education might make to the war effort. Thirdly, whatever Churchill thought, Butler was not displeased with the appointment. Indeed, the way he set about the task suggests he was strongly motivated, and that he quickly appreciated the potential of the post both for promoting Conservative reform and advancing his own career. He was, after all, only 38 and, having mentally prepared himself for political oblivion, any substantial post would no doubt have appealed to him.

Anthony Howard (Butler's official biographer) dismisses the idea that Churchill intended to insult Butler by offering the post. He also points out that Butler's contemporary note of the meeting with Churchill, made only a week or two later, provided the basis for the account in his autobiography (Howard, 1987, p. 109–10). It seems likely, therefore, that the account in the *Listener* was far less accurate and depended on Butler's memory of events twenty-five years earlier. Nevertheless, though Howard dismisses them as folklore, Churchill's remarks may well have been made in other meetings between the two around that time.

Whatever the truth of the matter, many observers considered it a setback for Butler. In the diary of the Conservative MP 'Chips' Channon, Butler's new post is described as 'a backwater'. The reputation of the Board of Education among politicians was not good. It was considered to be in the control of its permanent staff, for which, as we have seen, there was considerable evidence. Moreover, it had suffered from a lack of political status since Fisher's 1918 Act. For much of the inter-war period, it had been, as Sir John Simon described it, 'an outpost of the Treasury' (Middleton and Weitzman, 1976, p. 179). Butler's mentor, Lord Halifax, had held the post twice and had no doubt given him the lowdown. Halifax himself replying to John Simon had described the duty of the Board of Education as 'to pursue economies, having regard to the general exigencies of the public service in such a way that the system of education is not impaired'. This could have served as a motto for the rapid succession of ministers who held the post. There had been six presidents of the Board in the previous decade, averaging just over eighteen months each (as opposed to roughly two years each in the post-war period).

For Butler, being outside of Churchill's field of interest was a positive boon. A politician as astute as he was could make good use of the room for manoeuvre. It also provided him with an ideal place from which to drive forward the changes in Conservative party attitudes which he believed were so important to its future success. For the Board of Education and those interested in educational progress, Butler's appointment was a stroke of good fortune. Few politicians of the era could have seen through so major a set of reforms while the war continued to rage.

Privately, Butler made clear from the start his commitment to bringing about a 'reform representing the whole English character'. The day after his appointment he wrote to Chuter Ede of the 'opportunity we have to give the educational system . . . a real helping hand'. For this reason he was determined to find a means of extending the consultation beyond the limited number of organizations which had been sent the Green Book. Almost as soon as he began, however, he met with a setback: the Prime Minister.

In September 1941 Butler wrote to Churchill setting out the broad issues facing the Board, just as Churchill had suggested. The education and industrial sectors needed to be brought closer together, he argued, and solutions to the problems of industrial and technical training had to be found. Secondly, the Dual System and the role of the churches in education needed re-examination. Finally, the future of the public schools had to be considered. He therefore proposed to the Prime Minister the establishment of a joint select committee of both Houses of Parliament which would act as a tribunal, taking evidence from all the interested parties and developing solutions to the problems. Aware of Churchill's long political memory and sense of history, Butler argued that this proposal would enable them to avoid 'a dogfight in Parliament' and the difficulties created by the 1902 Education Act and its aftermath. It would prepare the ground for a government Bill at a later date and enable the 'harnessing [of] the spirit of the times to the course of social reform' (quoted in Howard, 1987).

Churchill's reply was uncompromising: 'I cannot contemplate a new Education Bill.' It would revive the terrible controversies over religion that had taken place earlier in the century and thereby detract from the war effort. Raising the public schools issue was equally dangerous. Instead, Butler should concentrate on getting 'the schools working as well as possible under all the difficulties of air attack, evacuation, etc.' (quoted in Howard, 1987). He could also consider how to improve industrial and technical training for future members of the armed forces. 'We cannot have party politics in war time,' he insisted.

Maurice Holmes tried rather weakly to comfort his new minister:

> I do not think we need be unduly cast down. There are, I feel, some advantages in our having more time than even your detailed programme contemplated for reaching the greatest common measure of agreement on the more contentious issues.
>
> (quoted *ibid.*, pp. 94–5)

Certainly Butler had been rebuffed, but he was not so easily deflected from the task he had set himself. Through Chuter Ede he sounded out Clement Attlee, who was the leader of the Labour Party, the Deputy Prime Minister and, given Churchill's commitment to the war, the single most influential figure on issues concerning the home front. Attlee thought the proposal for a joint select committee was politically inept, and to that extent confirmed Churchill's view. On the other hand, he urged Butler to go ahead with consultations with the churches and other interested parties. Attlee was a shrewd judge of such matters and Butler took his advice, not least because the only other option was to postpone reform indefinitely. Sir John Anderson, the Lord President, urged a similar course: consultations without controversy.

Butler learnt several lessons from the episode. One was that he could expect support from the Labour ministers whose enthusiasm for social reform was much greater than that of colleagues in his own party. As he wrote to a friend: 'I find that in education much of the drive . . . comes from Labour' (quoted in Jefferys, 1984). The second was that until he had a clear way through the controversies, Churchill should be left out of the equation, though his support, or at least his acquiescence, was ultimately essential. Thirdly, he needed to cultivate, gently, the support of other Conservative colleagues, particularly Anderson and Kingsley Wood, the Chancellor of the Exchequer. He set out, therefore, to resolve the religious issue and sidetrack the public schools question. With that accomplished, he might then go back to the Prime Minister with the hope of receiving a more positive reply. Apparently he wavered slightly, concerned about the ethics of proceeding in spite of the Prime Minister's express disapproval. Chuter Ede, a man renowned for his integrity, assured him he need have no qualms.

Suitably reassured, Butler turned to the most intractable problem: the Dual System which, as Frederick Mander, the NUT General Secretary, put it, lay 'like a tank trap across the highway to educational advance' (quoted in Barber, 1992, p. 31). It also obstructed the progress of Butler's career, so he had a double motive for solving the problem that had defied his predecessors for the previous fifty years.

BUTLER AND THE CHURCHES

Between his appointment in July 1941 and the passage of the Education Act three years later, Butler gave much more time and attention to the churches than to any other interested parties. Negotiations continued even while the Bill was working its way through Parliament.

It is important to clarify the stances taken by each of the main groups before examining in detail their negotiations with Butler. The Roman Catholics, who throughout proved the most difficult to negotiate with and the most intransigent, also faced the most severe difficulties financially. In February 1941 the Catholic Education Council had set out the parlous financial state they were in. It was impossible in these circumstances, they said, to contemplate ending all-through schools and completing the process of Hadow reorganization. Acknowledging the likelihood of pressure for change, they made clear that they could not accept educational reorganization without their 'knowledge, advice and consent' (Gosden, 1976).

A month before Butler's appointment, Cardinal Hinsley had taken a deputation to Ramsbotham and argued for a generous settlement. In response, Ramsbotham had made no firm commitments. He understood the need for public assistance to the Catholic schools, but stressed that this would imply a greater degree of public control. There would, he said, be further consultations. Broadly speaking, the battle lines were drawn. The Catholic hierarchy wanted the maximum financial assistance with the minimum loss of control. The Catholic religion's commitment to bringing up children in the faith meant that they clung to this view passionately. The hierarchical nature of the Roman Catholic Church meant, too, that they could mobilize their followers most effectively when they needed to do so.

The Church of England position was more complex, but also more flexible. As we saw earlier, many of its leading figures, and William Temple in particular, were deeply committed to the building of a New Jerusalem. The reform of the education system was an important part of this idealistic vision.

The New Jerusalem, as indeed the phrase suggests, was laced through with a commitment to promoting Christian faith both as a basis for policy and as a moral code for the whole of society. In the circumstances of war, it was the view of many that social reform, social solidarity and the Christian code of ethics marched together. *The Times*, that ardent advocate of educational reform, was also committed to extending religious influence. 'The future of religious education involves the future of our national life and character,' it asserted on 17 February 1940. Similarly, Sir Fred Clarke's advocacy of educational reform had always been underpinned by a commitment to Christianity: 'the aim of all education is the attainment of a right understanding of the eternal and the expression of that understanding in and through the ways of common life' (Clarke, 1923). This appears to have been an international trend in wartime. R. D. Baldwin argued in 1945 that, in the USA, 'the religious and spiritual impact may well be the most important of all those which the War will make upon the school' (Baldwin in Lowe, 1992, p. 55). It is in this context that 'The Five Points' issued from Lambeth Palace on 13 February 1941 should be understood. They asserted that:

- all children in all schools should receive a Christian education;
- religious education should be a recognized optional subject in training colleges;
- the statutory restriction that religion should be the first or last lesson in the day should be dropped;
- religious teaching should be inspected by HMI; and
- all schools should start the day with an Act of Worship.

These demands won widespread support both from traditionalists and those advocating reform. By July 1941, 224 MPs and peers had signed a declaration based on similar principles. One of Butler's first meetings as President of the Board was with the Archbishop of Canterbury about the Five Points. Butler was sympathetic but pointed out that the Church itself had a responsibility for religious education: it was not just a matter for the schools.

Unlike the Catholic Church, the Anglicans were prepared to consider a compromise involving greater state funding for church schools, in return for which the Church would cede a degree of control. At the meetings on 23 July and later in the year, they indicated that the Green Book's parameters for this compromise were broadly acceptable. They were keen, however, to see, as soon as possible, a single-clause Bill which would implement the five points. Butler and Ede resisted this, partly because they thought that if they agreed to it the Anglicans would lose interest in a sweeping reform, and partly because they believed, probably rightly, that such a Bill would provoke a bitter dispute about the Dual System, thus undermining their entire long-term plan. Instead, Butler and Ede agreed to circulate the five points so that they could be discussed at the same time as the Green Book.

The Nonconformists, or Free Churches, had interests radically different from those of both the Catholics and Anglicans. They had very few schools of their own, though that did not mean they were any less committed to the cause of education. The Methodists, for example, had chosen to invest in teacher training at colleges such as Westminster, rather than funding schools. They and others such as the Quakers had small numbers of independent schools which depended on fees rather than state funding.

It was the Nonconformists who had been so outraged by the sections in the 1902 Education Act which meant that Anglican and Catholic schools received state funding. Why should the propagation of those religions be subsidized by the state? Hence the famous slogan of the opposition to the 1902 Act, still embedded in the minds of many politicians, that it provided for 'Rome on the rates'. They hoped that any reform of the Dual System would ensure that state funding implied state control.

Within this general stance, the so-called 'single-school areas' were a particular grievance for the Nonconformists. In many rural areas, the only elementary school available was an Anglican one. Nonconformist parents understandably resented paying for (through their rates), and having to send their children to, an Anglican school. While, under the 1870 Cowper–Temple clause, they had the right as parents to withdraw their child from formal religious instruction, church schools nevertheless promoted an ethos throughout the school based on their religious beliefs. Nonconformist church leaders hoped to persuade the government to reform the situation radically in single-school areas; their preferred option would have been for church schools in such areas to be taken over by the local education authority. They were also keen to ensure that the Cowper–Temple clause was applied to all secondary schools. However, like many leaders of the Church of England, the leaders of the Free Churches were strongly committed to education reform and few of them would have wanted to scupper it through their own intransigence. This gave Butler sufficient room for manoeuvre with

Anglicans and Nonconformists to avoid the kind of damaging public rows that had taken place in 1902, and that, in the context of war, would have destroyed his reform proposals.

The Roman Catholics were a different case. Throughout Butler's painstaking efforts, he found they demanded the most time and energy for the least reward. They rejected the Green Book out of hand. Archbishop Hinsley claimed that it had severe flaws from the Roman Catholic point of view. It would cost more than the Roman Catholic community could conceivably afford to bring their schools up to standard and to reorganize all-age schools into primary and secondary schools. The result would be that all-age Roman Catholic schools would be decapitated by LEAs, thus losing their post-11 provision. Indeed, he argued, the proposals would effectively end the Dual System altogether. At meetings in the autumn of 1941, Butler and Ede made no progress, in spite of urging Hinsley and the other Catholics to take a positive approach. While the Catholic representatives accused the officials of being opposed to the Catholic cause, Maurice Holmes, in a note to Butler, described their attitude as 'simply silly' (quoted in Gosden, 1976).

If Butler and Ede made no progress in that quarter, they were able to find common ground elsewhere. The Anglicans and Free Church representatives pressed their respective viewpoints, but within a much more positive context than their Catholic counterparts. It was a major asset that Butler was a well-known Anglican and that Ede was a leading Nonconformist, and indeed a lay preacher. (His experience as a governor of a Jesuit school proved less useful.) Most important of all was the reputation for integrity that the ministerial pair developed. This enabled them to negotiate with all the interested parties without ever being suspected of being in the pocket of any one of them. Some of those most keenly interested in the religious issue were, of course, teachers and administrators.

The NUT, a long-standing champion of secondary education for all and of raising the school-leaving age, argued for the maintenance of the Cowper–Temple clause. It called for a guarantee that in any school which received state funding, religious instruction should be non-denominational and based on a nationally agreed syllabus. They also insisted that teachers should not be appointed on the basis of their religious beliefs.

The influential Association of Education Committees under Sir Percival Sharp wanted to see church schools transferred to the

LEAs, which, they argued, would increasingly have to pay for them. If this were done, they were happy to see denominational instruction in former church schools provided by reserved teachers (i.e. teachers appointed to specific posts which allowed for religious views to be taken into account). In all other schools, non-denominational religious education would be provided.

The Catholics' intransigence during that winter of 1941–42 brought them little benefit. The Board, instead, began to refine the proposals in line with those who had showed a willingness to negotiate, in particular the Nonconformists and teachers. The result, published just before Easter 1942, was the so-called White Memorandum. Politically, the key figure in its production was James Chuter Ede. Chuter Ede's role in the passage of the 1944 Education Act can hardly be overstated. He complemented Butler perfectly. He was a loyal Labour party politician who had been a member of Surrey County Council since 1914, and an MP in 1923, 1929–31 and from 1935 onwards. Later he would go on to become Home Secretary and briefly Leader of the House of Commons in the post-war Labour government. He had been an elementary-school teacher and an active member of the NUT. He thus had access not only to the national Labour politicians who exercised such a powerful influence on domestic affairs during the war, but to the Nonconformist and teacher leaders who were outside Butler's range of experience.

Ede was meticulous, thorough and a safe pair of hands. He also recorded all his activity in a twelve-volume diary which is housed in the British Library archives. He filled every page with neat script, leaving no space at the top or bottom and no more than a millimetre or so of margin. This may indicate a wartime concern for efficient use of resources; it also suggests a tidy mind, capable of mastering detail. The entries record not only the important business of the day, but also the train journeys in and out of Surrey, and his social engagements. If they are tedious reading in parts, their very thoroughness makes them an excellent historical source.

The White Memorandum of March 1942 was the government's second attempt at publishing proposals designed to solve the problems of the Dual System. It reflected the success of the Nonconformists' lobbying since the Green Book and, in particular, Chuter Ede's own personal preferences, as well as those of most board officials. It proposed that LEAs should take full responsibility for the supply of places in an area, and have power to decide the age range of schools and the organization of them. Two options were presented for the church schools. Under the first, they could be handed over to the LEA, with loss of control but with the right to use of the premises at weekends or other times when the buildings were not required for educational purposes. Church schools in single-school areas would be required to take this option.

Under the second option, available only in multi-school areas, voluntary schools would receive a 50 per cent grant for building repairs, and the LEA would pay the running costs of the school in full. In return, the LEA would have responsibility for, and control of, secular instruction. The managers of the school would appoint staff and control religious instruction. In the case of either option, the Cowper–Temple clause would apply.

In the second option, the White Memorandum foreshadowed what, in the 1944 Act itself, became voluntary-aided status. The first option, by contrast, was buried under the weight of opposition from the Church of England and its friends in the Conservative party.

As Sir Percival Sharp and his colleagues pointed out on 19 March 1942, it was the Church of England which stood to lose most if the White Memorandum were implemented, since almost all the voluntary schools in single-school areas were theirs. Indeed, 4,000 of their 10,000 schools were in single-school areas. While the Nonconformists were delighted with the Memorandum, the Church of England rejected its proposals. When Butler, ever the pragmatic politician, received a firmly negative telephone call from a leading Tory and Anglican grandee, Lord Selborne, he knew the White Memorandum was dead: 'from that time on, I knew it would be necessary to adjust this scheme,' he recorded later (quoted in Gosden, 1976, p. 278). Meanwhile, the Catholics rejected it too. For them, the second option offered too little cash. In fact, Butler had kept the grant as low as 50 per cent so as to be able to make a concession to the Catholics at a later stage in the negotiations. At this point, though, he kept his cards close to his chest.

The White Memorandum was, however, not without its benefits. It assisted the NUT Executive in swinging the union's conference that Easter behind a pragmatic position on the reform of the Dual System. It also gave greater urgency to the discussions between the Board and the Church of England.

A series of meetings between Butler and Archbishop Temple took place in the ensuing months. The relationship between the two was extremely important; the degree of trust enabled them to explore possibilities without being tied into positions. From Temple's point of view, the White Memorandum's proposals for single-school areas were impossible. Great though his respect for Butler was, this was too much. In any case, he had to bring the Church with him. On 5 June 1942 Butler received a formal deputation from the Church of England. Sympathetic but firm, he revealed to them the unacceptable state of the church schools. The status quo was impossible, and if the state was to foot a large part of the bill for the repair of these buildings, then it had a right to some measure of control.

A month later Temple showed Butler, in confidence, the first draft of a policy proposal which he intended to put before the Church of England assembly that autumn. This argued that the five points should be seen as an addition rather than an alternative to the Dual System. It accepted the idea of an agreed syllabus for religious education on condition that the managers of a voluntary school could supplement it if they chose. Finally it accepted that LEAs could appoint teachers, as long as the school managers could keep control of the appointment of teachers of religious instruction. In return, the upkeep and running costs of the schools would transfer to the LEA.

Here was the germ of the idea that, in the Act, became the voluntary-controlled option.

Butler, aware of the pressure Temple might come under at his assembly, now made concessions in return. By September the Board had made it clear publicly that the White Memorandum had been dropped. In the same month, another Church of England deputation was offered the voluntary-aided option (the White Memorandum's second option) and the voluntary-controlled option which emanated from Temple's proposals. They were also offered financial assistance to complete the 11–14 senior schools which had begun after the 1936 Act. In October, over lunch, Butler and Temple agreed to reject the NUT's proposal for a nationally agreed syllabus for religious education.

Enough had now been done for Temple to gain the support of the assembly in spite of opposition from the Bishop of Chichester and others. This represented a triumph for Butler and Temple. Privately, Butler acknowledged the courage and foresight Temple had shown, but at Temple's request he said nothing in public about the informal pact between them.

The importance of their success during 1942 should not be underestimated. As far as the Church of England was concerned, the road to the 1944 Act was now clear. This was not all; squaring the Church of England greatly improved the chances of Butler winning support from fellow Conservative cabinet members and the massed ranks of the Tory back benches.

When Butler met the home front ministers they were enthusiastic. Butler's estimate that only 500 or so of the Church of England's 10,000 schools would qualify for the voluntary-aided option encouraged them further. Outside the meeting, Kingsley Wood, the Chancellor of the Exchequer, expressed his personal support for Butler's efforts. He was encouraged by the fact that the achievement of education reform began relatively cheaply, though it became progressively more expensive. Wood, with firm backing from Churchill, was vigilant in resisting commitments that could lead to unspecified expenditure immediately after the war. His support for Butler was therefore politically essential. According to Butler, in his informal remarks, he 'went so far as to say that he would rather give the money for education than throw it down the sink with Sir William Beveridge' (14 September 1942). Politically, Butler was able to exploit this favourable comparison with the ageing self-publicist and Liberal Sir William Beveridge, whose plans for a national system of social security outraged the Prime Minister and were anathema to the Treasury.

During October Butler won approval for his plans from the Free Church Federal Council, the Association of Education Committees and the National Union of Teachers. The latter was anxious about the influence of denominational issues on the appointment of head-teachers, and teachers under the voluntary-aided option. They were promised that a clause in the Bill would guarantee that no teacher should suffer professional disadvantage for denominational reasons. There was a distant echo of this promise when, after hearing the views of NUT officials in September 1992, the government included a similar clause in the very different 1993 Education Act.

Meanwhile, the Roman Catholics, in spite of Butler's efforts, remained irreconcilable. During the summer of 1942, Butler made little progress in his efforts to build a serious negotiating relationship with the Catholic Church. Eventually he met Archbishop Hinsley in August and listened while the Archbishop urged the adoption of the Scottish solution. This involved generous state aid to Catholic schools without requiring them to swallow much in the way of state control. Butler had done his homework. This 'solution' was unrealistically expensive. It involved offering the churches a blank cheque, which in wartime in particular would be irresponsible. In any case, Butler's meticulous approach involved presenting himself to his Conservative cabinet colleagues as sober and responsible in the cause of reform. Furthermore, Butler was also aware that the Scottish option would result in huge political controversy. The free churches, the teacher organizations and the local authorities would be inflamed. It was not only that Butler was keen to see a judicious compromise; it was also that he knew the whole enterprise of reform would be sunk if the Prime Minister caught a whiff of a rekindled row over 'Rome on the rates'. The Scottish option was therefore a non-runner.

On 15 September Butler outlined the two practical options to a Roman Catholic deputation, and suggested that the voluntary-aided option might suit them best. The Catholic representatives, however, felt that the 50 per cent grant was insufficient. For the moment, Butler was not prepared to offer any more, and the meeting broke up inconclusively. There were further meetings from time to time during the autumn and winter, but the Catholics showed little sign of compromise. The grant in the voluntary-aided option was too low; the proposed agreed syllabus was unacceptable. Worse still, Butler was unable to build up the kind of relationship with the leaders of the Catholic Church that he had achieved so effectively with Archbishop Temple. Indeed, it seemed to be part of the Catholics' tactics to be nebulous. The only concession Butler was prepared to envisage was improving the 50 per cent grant for those senior schools that followed reorganization under the 1936 Act.

On 15 January 1943, Butler met Hinsley and made clear his frustration at the lack of progress. If the NUT and other supporters of reform were to be kept behind his plans, urgent progress towards a Bill was needed. He repeated that the 100 per cent grant that the Catholics wanted was politically out of the question. An increase to 75 per cent for new senior schools might be considered. His pleas made no impact. When the Catholics brought a formal deputation on 3 February, led this time by Archbishop Downey, they remained implacable. The gap was as great as ever. Butler even visited Scotland to explore the issue in greater depth. His views were reinforced rather than altered. In Scotland, over 50 per cent of schoolteachers were subject to denominational tests; this would be anathema to the NUT which, from its foundation in 1870, had fundamentally opposed such tests.

Butler felt by early 1943 that there was little more he could do to settle with the Catholics. Politically it was important that he had been seen to seek a settlement, and that it was intransigence on the side of the Catholic Church which was perceived as preventing agreement. This he had achieved. Since he had also found a compromise which had won the backing of the Church of England, the Nonconformists and the teachers, he believed he was in a position to forge ahead. The Catholics, as it turned out, remained opposed to Butler's plans throughout 1943 and even during the passage of the Act. Politically, however, their opposition could be discounted since Butler's carefully constructed compromise ensured their isolation.

BUTLER AND LOCAL GOVERNMENT REORGANIZATION

At the outbreak of war there had been 315 local education authorities in England and Wales. Of these, 169 were so-called 'Part III' authorities, which had responsibility solely for elementary education. In addition, there were 63 county councils and 83 county boroughs which had responsibility for both elementary and secondary education. This complex pattern was further complicated by the fact that while London and 16 other counties had no Part III authorities, others had many. Middlesex, for example, had 12 and Lancashire had as many as 27.

The Part III authorities were not simply administratively untidy; they had significant problems. They found it harder to recruit good administrative staff and new teachers. They had also been less effective in bringing about Hadow-style reorganization. These were minor problems, however, compared to their incompatibility with the idea of secondary education for all. It was this in particular that had led the authors of the Green Book to recommend a single type of authority. In this, they were simply repeating a position taken up by most of the major reports of the inter-war period. As we have seen, however, the Green Book's authors felt it would be stepping outside their remit to suggest how a single type of authority should be achieved, since it had implications for the organization of local government as a whole.

One option open to Butler and Ede was the idea of a full-scale inquiry into the whole question of local government. As they had discovered by setting up the Fleming Committee to look at the public schools question, this was an attractive means of keeping a divisive question off the agenda for a while. The Association of Metropolitan Counties proposed just such a 'full and impartial inquiry'. The problem was that it would have caused a lengthy delay to the whole reform process since local government was critical to the implementation of any proposals. Butler and Ede could not, therefore, countenance it.

In fact, Sir William Jowitt, the Paymaster-General, and other government ministers had considered the possibility of an inquiry for other reasons, but ruled it out, not least because the developing thinking on health reform implied a need for very large authorities.

The County Councils Association accepted the need for a single type of authority, knowing that its members would benefit from movement towards the idea. The position of the Association of Education Committees (AEC) was a different matter altogether. Although the AEC brought together representatives from all types of education authority, simple numbers gave the Part III authorities a predominant voice in its affairs. It therefore defended their role and argued that there should be no significant changes until the whole question of local government after the war had been resolved. Needless to say, the Federation of Part III Authorities took an even stronger line against the Board, arguing that they should have their responsibilities extended to include the provision of post-primary education.

The board officials had never considered this to be a serious option. The Part III authorities were mostly too small to be able to bring about the coherent structure of secondary provision that the Green Book envisaged. The NUT and the other teacher organizations agreed. They wanted all-purpose LEAs and the abolition of most Part III authorities, with possibly some of the large Part III authorities being given full powers.

Butler and his colleagues, keen to drive reform through during the war, developed a practical solution of their own. For this they had the backing of the crucial War Cabinet Committee on Reconstruction. The counties and county boroughs would become all-purpose LEAs. The Part III authorities would lose their role, but they would be appeased by the LEAs being given the power to delegate authority to Part III districts within their borders, and by the larger Part III authorities having the right of representation on LEA education committees.

Within the government, the issues continued to be debated. Ede urged the idea of local sub-committees under the Local Government Act of 1929. Holmes and his officials, on the other hand, were opposed to conceding too much to former Part III LEAs, which they saw as a vested interest standing in the way of progress. On the whole, in the White Paper the officials had their way.

The interests of the Part III authorities, however, had powerful advocates. Sir Percival Sharp of the AEC was a formidable spokesperson and a power in the land. Indeed, he was so firmly committed to the status quo that he ruled out even proposing alternatives, which he said would be 'equivalent to running up the White Flag'. When he met Butler and Ede in May 1943, he asked for a specific assurance that the local interest would be recognized and room provided for local initiative. He wanted Part III authorities to retain their powers and make appointments to the higher (i.e. secondary) education committees of the counties. In reply, Butler – his eye on the ball, as ever – argued that he was determined to take advantage of the circumstances and make real progress while he had the chance. For this reason, he ruled out any inquiry; he rejected, too, the suggestion that the kind of coherent reform of secondary education he envisaged could be achieved if the existing powers of Part III authorities were left untouched. Butler, therefore, made no concessions. Sharp and his colleagues, however, kept up the pressure, and won, as we shall see, some modest but significant concessions in the period between the White Paper and the Bill.

BUTLER AND THE EDUCATION REFORMS

So far this substantial chapter on Butler's impact on the reform process has said little about his views on education reform. It has concentrated on his political impact, his tortuous negotiations with the churches and his less tortuous progress on the local government question. While clearly his views on education reform are important, the chapter nevertheless gives a fair reflection of his impact, not least because to a very large extent the Green Book had settled most of the important educational issues in a way which made broad consensus possible. Out in the country there was considerable pressure to go further faster, but so parched was the thirst of those who favoured education reform that, on the whole, they were prepared to compromise as long as the dream of secondary education for all was achieved. Nevertheless, some of the issues continued to be debated after the Green Book and the appointment of Butler, both within the Board and in the country.

The issue of multilateral schools within the Board was kept alive partly as a result of pressure from Graham Savage, Education Officer of London County Council. He set out the standard case against the tripartite division of secondary education, adding that in practice it would prove difficult to rectify errors in the allocation of children to schools after the age of 11. History would bear him out on this point. He also argued, less plausibly, that once a school was larger than 250 it would seem large anyway and that therefore schools of 2,000 to 2,500 would be acceptable. In the spring of 1942, R. S. Wood initiated further discussion within the Board on the organization of secondary schools. Neither the secondary nor the technical branch had moved any closer to Cleary and the elementary branch. In the country, the issue continued to be debated.

Butler himself eventually took a personal interest in the issue. Evidently he was concerned about irrevocable decisions affecting individual children being made at 11 plus: 'I am not satisfied that the age of 11 is the one and ideal age at which children should decide their future lives' (Butler to Holmes, 20 October 1942). Butler was sufficiently concerned to read the exchange on the issue between the officials during the preparation of the Green Book: 'How do we propose to arrange for the re-switch between 11 and 13 if we don't have multilateral schools?' (*ibid.*, 26 February 1943). Reassurance came from Barrow, the Secretary of the Norwood Committee and an arch-advocate of the tripartite system. Allocation at 11 would only be 'a rough shake out' (a phrase which, with hindsight, looks distinctly unreassuring). Each secondary school, Barrow maintained, would have a lower school from 11 to 13 with a similar curriculum. It must be assumed that Butler was sufficiently convinced by these exchanges in early 1943 to leave the matter alone.

Butler took a similar interest in the question of the direct-grant schools. There was widespread criticism, from social reformers in the country, of the Green Book's proposal to allow direct-grant schools to continue to charge fees on the doubtful grounds that 'to deprive them of their fee income would mean their disappearance' (Board of Education, 1941, p. 398).

Butler sympathized with the idea of abolishing fees in the day direct-grant schools, but the issue divided the Conservative party. Conservative representatives of LEAs generally took the view that the direct-grant schools should be absorbed within the LEA system as highly academic grammar schools. Many Tory MPs, however, particularly if they had a direct-grant school in their constituency, favoured the status quo. The Conservative party's Education Committee, which Butler found embarrassingly reactionary, agreed. In the end, Butler, conscious as ever of the need to ensure party unity in Parliament, left the Green Book's proposals intact. Indeed, publicly he became an enthusiast for them, arguing that he did not want 'all schools *gleichgeschaltet* [made equal, or brought into line], I prefer a shading off'. The use of the German word, with its inevitable Nazi connotations during wartime, suggests that ultimately he was strongly behind maintaining the status of the direct-grant schools.

With regard to part-time day continuation schools too, Butler maintained the position of the Green Book. There was little ideological opposition to the proposal for those between 15 and 18 to receive part-time education. It had been legislated for in 1918, only to have been killed off in practice by the financial retrenchment of the inter-war years. In order to avoid such a failure again, Butler took the view that the legislation should include an 'appointed day' from when provision should be made. The County Councils Association was anxious about the implications of this for capital expenditure since its members believed they did not have sufficient buildings ready. Ernest Bevin, a staunch ally of Butler's efforts in the Cabinet, was doubtful for a different reason. He thought that if 15–18 day continuation schools were provided, it would result in the postponement of the introduction of a school-leaving age of 16. Unless that were achieved at the end of the war, it would, he forecast, not happen for twenty years. In fact, as we now know, it had to wait even longer. Ironically, and with devastating consequences from which we are still suffering, the proposal for day continuation schools, though it survived firmly in the White Paper and in the Education Act, never came to fruition either.

On two other education issues of crucial importance Butler established inquiries in order to enable him to focus on what he perceived to be the all-important structural issues. Both the Fleming Committee on the future of the public schools and the Norwood Committee on secondary curriculum and examinations played a critical role in enabling Butler to put his Act on the statute book.

The Fleming Committee was set up 'to consider means whereby the association between the public schools . . . and the general education system of the country could be extended and developed' (Board of Education, 1944a, Terms of Reference). There was considerable popular demand for the old public school system to be dismantled. There was a powerful feeling both that its elitism was inconsistent with the social cohesion of wartime and that it was partly responsible for the disastrous course of the war in its first year or so.

Though Butler recognized the strength of this body of opinion, he also knew his own party in Parliament. The swathes of back-benchers elected in 1935, and marginalized by the centralization of the political process in wartime, would rise almost to a man to defend the schools that had educated them. The Fleming Committee was the ideal way of shifting the issue off the agenda, out of the White Paper and out of the Bill. As Butler so succinctly put it in his autobiography, 'the first class carriage had been shunted into an immense siding' (Butler, 1971, p. 120). The committee moved slowly and produced, for publication in the same month as the 1944 Act hit the statute book, what Butler described as a 'sensationally disingenuous report' proposing nothing more than the idea of state-funded bursaries to support 'qualified' pupils for up to 25 per cent of places in public schools. This idea had in any case been advocated by some of the public schools themselves on the eve of war to help them out of their financial woes. The Assisted Places Scheme established by the Thatcher government in 1980 was a refinement of the Fleming recommendation.

Politically, the establishment of the committee did its job. All Butler had to do while it deliberated was explain that he was awaiting its findings, and make sure in the mean time that the diehards in the benches behind him kept a low profile. When the reactionary Conservative Education Committee proposed to publish a document promoting the public schools, Butler intervened successfully to persuade them that silence would serve their interests better.

The Norwood Committee served a different purpose, but to equally good effect from Butler's point of view. Once the idea of secondary education for all was universally accepted, as it was by 1941, then the question of the secondary curriculum could hardly be postponed. By establishing the Norwood Committee to look into it, Butler simultaneously removed another potential minefield from the political agenda for the mean time, and also ensured that the tripartite division of secondary schooling would find an ideological underpinning. No wonder Brian Simon describes its establishment as 'a masterstroke'.

As early as 31 January 1940, the issue of the post-war curriculum had been vigorously raised by Geoffrey Vickers in the influential *Christian Newsletter*. In a wide-ranging article entitled 'Educating for a Free Society' he asked:

> What should be the content of education and what its object? What should be the place and scope of religious teaching? Apart from religious teaching, how can the schools best contribute to the training of character? . . . What is the educative value of collective activities and in what sort of communities should children experience them?
>
> The issues are much wider than the domain of education. They go to the root of the question – for what are we trying to educate? In what kind of world do we expect them to live? . . . It is time to face these controversies, for education more than any other social activity can shape the future, and Britain is bound to be faced with the need for radical re-shaping.

Indeed, in 1943, Harold Dent, editor of the *Times Educational Supplement*, was arguing that the whole reform process was impoverished because it neglected these wider and deeper questions and focused almost entirely on structural issues. Professional opinion had 'taken its cue from the political platform,' he argued, and though it 'has succeeded in achieving a remarkable unanimity of opinion on a great many important questions, chiefly in the sphere of structural reform, . . . it has hardly begun to touch the fundamental problems of education in a democratic society' (Dent, 1943, p. 167).

It is easy to see how Butler, the pragmatic politician, would shy away from opening up such wide-ranging questions, with the danger of the whole process spiralling out of political control. It is easy to see too how the leaders of the profession – Ronald Gould and others – would want to promote a more sharply focused debate while leaving teachers in control of the curriculum. Yet, with hindsight again, it is noticeable how the lack of clarity in the profession about the role of the curriculum in a democracy left it open to the onslaught of the late 1980s. Fascinatingly, during the process of debating the curriculum, particularly in the run-up to Sir Ron Dearing's review, these questions were at last receiving credible professional answers.

In 1941, however, Butler was convinced that curriculum issues were better dealt with by the Norwood committee. It was, in fact, an unusual committee. Officially it was a sub-committee of the Secondary Schools Examinations Council (SSEC). In practice it answered directly to Butler and the Board of Education. When the SSEC protested at the fact that it received copies of the Norwood Committee's report only after it had gone to Butler, its objections were, as Brian Simon puts it, unceremoniously dismissed.

The key to its proposals lay in its membership and its staffing. Sir Cyril Norwood, its chair, was an enlightened but conservative former headmaster of Harrow, and now Master of a Cambridge college. G. G. Williams, the Board of Education's overt elitist, was involved not only in picking the members of the committee, but directly in its deliberations. Its conclusions strongly endorsed the tripartite system. On 31 July 1943 the *TES* admirably summarized its recommendations:

> It is administratively impossible to offer individual curricula; school organisation must assume that individuals have enough in common to justify certain rough groupings. Three main groupings appear desirable: of pupils interested in learning for its own sake; pupils whose interests and abilities are markedly in the field of applied science or applied art; and pupils who deal more easily with concrete things than with ideas.
>
> To meet the respective needs of these groupings, the committee envisages three broad types of secondary education, and consequently three types of secondary school: grammar, technical and modern.
>
> (p. 365)

Butler commented in a note to Holmes and Williams shortly before its publication that 'this well-written report will serve our book very well – particularly its layout of the secondary world' (Butler to Holmes and Williams, 6 June 1943).

When the report was published, ten days after the great 1943 White Paper, it received warm endorsement. The *TES* described it as 'a very valuable document not only because of the changes . . . which it recommends but also because of the philosophy of education developed and defined in its pages' (editorial, 31 July 1943, p. 367). But it was not without its critics. Their views were summarized later by the historian S. J. Curtis, who unerringly found the Report's weakness: 'The suggestion of the Committee seems to be that the Almighty has benevolently created three types of child in just those proportions which would gratify education administrators' (Curtis, 1952, pp. 114–15). Julian Huxley, writing in the *TES* soon after the report's publication, argued that it virtually denied 'social relevance and . . . the social function of education' and that its proposals were 'vicious, they need reformulation by those who think in terms of facilitating social change instead of (perhaps unconsciously) resisting it' (*TES*, 28 July 1943, p. 412).

In 1943 it did its job very effectively, justifying the chief proposals in the White Paper, *Educational Reconstruction*, which had just been published (Board of Education, 1943a). The road to legislation was clear. Butler must have felt very satisfied, for it was as a result of his political acumen that all the obstacles along its way had been removed.

Chapter 4

Parliament

A Happy New Year. . . . Everyone hopes, and believes, that 1944 will
see the end of the war in Europe and the beginning of a new era in
Western Civilisation.

Times Educational Supplement, 1 January 1944

THE WHITE PAPER AND ITS RECEPTION

On Friday, 16 July 1943, Butler's White Paper, *Educational Reconstruction*, was finally published. It had been widely anticipated that
Butler's plans would be published in the form of a Bill, but his concern for meticulous political preparation suggested that a White
Paper followed by a Bill would be a better course. That way the
consensus he had brought about on the structure of the education
system and the political support he had drawn together in the War
Cabinet could be consolidated. As he explained in presenting the
White Paper to the House, 'It is the desire of the Government that
ample opportunity should be given for consideration of the plan
as set out in the White Paper, before the stage of legislation is
reached' (Hansard, 16 July 1943).

This approach also gave him further opportunity to refine the
proposals on the Dual System and the Part III authorities
which were most likely to prove contentious. The White Paper,
however, would increase the pressure on his critics – especially the
Catholic Church – and ensure that he, not they, had the initiative
in the negotiations which ensued. This was particularly the case
after the overwhelmingly enthusiastic response his White Paper
received.

The *TES* editorial opened:

A landmark has been set up in English education. The government's
White Paper promises the greatest and grandest educational advance
since 1870. It offers a framework within which it will be possible

to achieve almost all the reforms on which the main body of instructed opinion is agreed.

It continued:

> However much some may feel that here and there the White Paper does not go far or fast enough, it must be acknowledged – and handsomely – that the Government have made a very substantial stride towards securing 'for children a happier childhood and a better start in life'.
>
> > (*TES*, 24 July 1943, p. 355)

The Times agreed:

> For the first time since 1870, an Education Bill is projected which is not a rewriting of a previous Act. The overlappings and inconsistencies of the existing system are largely swept away and replaced by an original layout based on a new and fundamentally sound principle.
>
> > (*The Times*, quoted in *Education*, 23 July 1943)

The *Guardian* was enthusiastic too:

> The Board, with Mr Butler at its head, has sounded advance all along the line.
>
> > (*Guardian*, quoted *ibid.*)

Education itself, through Sir Percival Sharp's caustic week-by-week column, subjected the White Paper to a searching but supportive critique, targeting in particular its proposals for local government and its financial provisions. Nevertheless, his opening comments are congratulatory:

> Even those who differ from [Mr Butler] on important detail will not withhold tribute to the care, courage and vision which mark his first venture as a responsible Minister in the field of big legislation.
>
> > (*ibid.*, p. 99)

The interest groups were broadly positive too. In its Executive Statement on the White Paper, the NUT welcomed its publication and recorded their pleasure at learning that the government intended 'to legislate for a far reaching measure of post-war educational reform'. The only fierce opposition came, inevitably enough, from the Roman Catholic Church. The Archbishop of Birmingham commented:

> The present English educational system provides schools built with public money for those who are satisfied with undenominational

religious teaching . . . but it refuses to provide schools for those who
cannot in conscience accept this. . . . This amounts to a refusal to
give our children equal opportunity of education.
(Address at St Philip's Grammar School, Edgbaston, 21 July 1943)

Other than the Catholics, the chief line of criticism was from those
who were impatient for change, and found the timetable and financial plans inadequate. This comes through powerfully in the TUC
Report of 1943:

This [White Paper] ill fits the necessities and the temper of the
times, and lags a long way behind public opinion which is eager that
the opportunity of restructuring our educational system should be
grasped now.
(TUC Report 1943, quoted in Simon, 1991, p. 70)

Overall, H. C. Dent, writing shortly after its publication, summarized views on the government's document. The White Paper's
proposals:

exceeded almost everyone's expectations. Not because there was anything novel about the proposals, nor because these went further in
the direction of change than had generally been urged; but because
they were built round a central and fundamental proposal which
involved a complete re-casting of the entire educational set-up, gave
unity to the educational system and an enhanced value to all the
other proposals.
(Dent, 1943, p. 223)

Its coherence and the comprehensive nature of its proposals were
indeed the White Paper's most striking features. Looking back,
however, through the haze of more recent Education White Papers,
which read like party political tracts, what is most striking is the
balanced discussion of issues and the sober clarity with which conclusions are drawn.

The White Paper begins with a quotation from Disraeli: 'Upon
the education of the people of this country the fate of this country
depends.' The choice of a quotation from a Conservative politician,
at once a proud nationalist and radical social reformer, was
judicious in the circumstances, and provides further evidence of
Butler's astute political judgement.

The introduction then sets out its philosophical underpinning.
The government had three purposes, it argued:

to secure for children a happier childhood and a better start in life;
to ensure a fuller measure of education and opportunity for young

people and to provide a means for all of developing the various talents with which they are endowed and so enriching the inheritance of the country whose citizens they are.

(White Paper, p. 3)

Education was not to be seen as shaping children so much as giving them the power to shape society. Children are to be subjects not objects, and in first place is the goal of a happier childhood.

'The new educational opportunities must not, therefore, be of a single pattern,' the Introduction continued. And then, in a passage which anticipated the debate which would surround John Patten's *Choice and Diversity* almost fifty years later, it urged:

It is just as important to achieve diversity as it is to ensure equality of educational opportunity. But such diversity must not impair the social unity which will open the way to a more closely knit society.

(*ibid.*)

In other words, diversity should be limited by the need for social cohesion, not allowed to run riot. In 1944 diversity was important, but no more so than equality of opportunity.

In order to secure these overarching ends and to ensure that the youth of the nation is developed 'to the greatest advantage', the White Paper proposed 'to recast the national education service':

The new layout is based on a recognition of the principle that education is a continuous process conducted in successive stages. For children below the compulsory school age of 5 there must be a sufficient supply of nursery schools. The period of compulsory school attendance will be extended to 15 without exemptions and with provision for its extension to 16 as soon as circumstances permit. The period from 5 to the leaving age will be divided into two stages, the first, to be known as primary, covering the years up to about 11. After 11 secondary education, of diversified types but on equal standing, will be provided for all children. At the primary stage the large classes and bad conditions which at present are a reproach to many elementary schools will be systematically eliminated; at the secondary stage, the standard of accommodation and amenities will be steadily raised to the level of the best examples.

(*ibid.*)

Here it is: the bold outline of a school system which reformers had advocated for so long. The opening paragraphs of the White Paper ring with confidence, perhaps bordering on the idealistic. For this was not all.

> When the period of full-time compulsory schooling ends, the young person will continue under educational influences up to 18 years of age either by remaining in full-time attendance at a secondary school, or by part-time day attendance at a young person's college. . . . Opportunities for technical and adult education will be increased.
>
> (*ibid.*)

Ambitious though this scheme was, the Introduction makes plain that this will not happen all at once. Here simultaneously was an important note of realism and a nod in the direction of the watchful eye of the Treasury:

> The introduction of each portion of the plan will be related to an Appointed Day. In this way it will be possible to fit these schemes for educational reform into the general picture of social reconstruction and to introduce the various portions of the plan as and when the necessary buildings, the equipment and the teachers become available.
>
> (*ibid.*, p. 4)

It was recognized that the proposal would involve a steady increase in the burden on the taxpayer and ratepayer over a series of years. The country's resources would be under severe pressure after the war: 'The rate of development of the proposals will therefore have to be determined from time to time in the light of these considerations' (*ibid.*).

The argument is not left here. The White Paper identifies the putting in place of the new structure, the raising of the school-leaving age to 15 and the part-time 15–18 places as matters that would be prioritized, 'to be undertaken immediately after the war', as part of the Prime Minister's recently announced four-year plan. Interestingly, the White Paper sets out in an appendix the anticipated cost of its proposals for the seven years after the war and the way in which the burden would be shared between central and local government. Though what actually happened fell far short of what was envisaged, it is a tribute to the thoroughness of planning that characterized the Board's preparation for education reform. It also provided the necessary information for an informed debate to take place in the service about the financing of reform and thus contributed in a significant way to democratic accountability. The absence of such a debate in 1988 or 1993 highlights the quality of the 1943 White Paper. The statement in the 1992 White Paper that its proposals would have no effect on overall education expenditure simply revealed its lack of ambition.

The Introduction of *Educational Reconstruction* concludes with an assertion that legislation alone will not bring about the desired progress: 'Ultimately the extent of the advance will depend upon the character of the schools, the nature of their life and work and the capacities of the teachers.' In spite of these difficulties, the government would not delay legislation because it would not wish 'dangerously to postpone plans for the vast majority of children. . . . Nor would it wish to ignore the broad measure of agreement which exists . . . upon the wide field covered by this Paper' (*ibid.*, p. 4). In 1943, the government – as a result of the hard work of Butler and Ede – knew that to be true. In 1992 it was not true, and no effort was made to achieve a broad measure of agreement of any kind.

The second section of the White Paper concentrates on full-time schooling. It begins by identifying the defects of the pre-war system, and condemns as inadequate its aim, as set down in the 1921 Education Act, 'to cause that child to receive efficient elementary instruction in reading, writing and arithmetic'. It condemns indeed the whole idea of 'elementary education', a term which vanished from the English education system with the 1944 Act. Worse still, 'it is now generally accepted that 14 is too early . . . for full-time schooling to cease, as it does at present for 90% of the children' (*ibid.*, p. 5).

Further flaws are identified: the separation of elementary from secondary education for administrative purposes; the Dual System; the inadequate provision of nursery education, given that in 1939 only 10,000 children aged 2–5 were in nursery schools and 166,000 aged 3–5 in nursery classes. While infant schools were 'among the most successful of the publicly provided schools', the junior schools were the 'Cinderellas' (Key Stage 2, it seems, has always been difficult). Class sizes are far too high, it argues. A teacher with fifty in a class cannot succeed and is engaged in 'not education but mass production' (*ibid.*, pp. 5–6).

Transition to secondary education is the biggest fault line, it claims, with only 9.5 per cent going to secondary school and the rest either in separate senior elementary schools or in the upper classes of the all-age schools they attend. Moreover, this selection process depends upon an examination. 'There is nothing to be said in favour of a system which subjects children at the age of 11 to the strain of a competitive examination on which, not only their future schooling, but their future careers may depend.' Furthermore, these examinations mean that 'the curriculum is too often cramped and distorted by over-emphasis on examination subjects' (*ibid.*, p. 6).

The fact that less than 50 per cent of children were in schools reorganized after Hadow is condemned, and the charging of fees is described as offending 'against the canon that the nature of a child's education should be determined by his capacity and promise and not by the financial circumstances of his parent' (*ibid.*, p. 7). In short, comprehensive reform is required. The White Paper goes on to describe the reforms it envisages for the schools sector:

> It will be organised in three progressive stages to be known as primary education, secondary education and further education.
>
> (*ibid.*, p. 7)

This sentence alone was immensely significant in its time.

Each LEA will be given a duty:

> to contribute towards the mental, moral and physical development of the community by securing the provision of efficient education throughout those stages for all persons in the area capable of profiting thereby.
>
> (*ibid.*)

The LEA therefore was to be the powerhouse of the Butler reforms.

> For the fulfilment of the duties . . . Local Education Authorities will be required to make a comprehensive survey of the existing provision and the present and prospective needs of their areas and to prepare and submit to the Board development plans which will give a complete picture of the proposed layout of primary and secondary schools.
>
> (*ibid.*)

These plans were required to show what was needed to bring all schools – provided and non-provided – up to the standards of the Board's regulations. Once the Board had approved the plan, it would make an education order for that area specifying the steps the LEA would have to take to bring about its reorganization and a timetable for these to be undertaken. In short, an ordered administrative revolution was planned; the decision-making would be shared between local and central government; implementation would be almost entirely a local affair.

At the same time, the parent's duty would be widened. The 'three Rs' would no longer be enough. The parent's duty would be 'to cause his child to receive efficient full-time education suitable to the child's age and aptitude' (*ibid.*, p. 8). Having explained how its reforms would be brought about, the White Paper then details its proposals for each phase of education.

For nursery education, it is proposed that the Board will take a power to prescribe the extent of nursery education in each LEA. The conditions revealed in large cities during the evacuation are cited to justify expansion:

> There is no doubt of the importance of training children in good habits at the most impressionable age and of the indirect value of the nursery school in influencing the parents of the children.
>
> (*ibid.*, p. 8)

The White Paper indicated a preference for nursery schools because they provide 'a more suitable environment, are nearer to the homes . . . and give less opportunity for the spread of infectious diseases' (*ibid.*).

The plans for infant and junior schools are based on the premise that separate infant and junior schools are preferable. It is argued that the reform of secondary education will enable junior schools 'to devote themselves to their proper task', instead, presumably, of cramming children in preparation for selective examinations. Needless to say, there is a much longer section on secondary schooling. In view of what became the practice in the 1950s and 1960s, it is worth quoting the White Paper's proposals for classifying children appropriately for the three types of secondary school:

> children at about the age of 11 should be classified, not on the results of a competitive test, but on an assessment of their individual aptitudes largely by such means as school records, supplemented, if necessary, by intelligence tests, due regard being had to their parents' wishes and the careers they have in mind.
>
> (*ibid.*, p. 9)

In other words, professional judgement was to take centre stage, with the intelligence test as a supplement. A question of major significance, in view of the debate in the early 1990s, is why teachers in the 1950s and 1960s surrendered their professional judgement to the all-consuming 11-plus.

The White Paper explains that transfer between 11 and 13 will be allowed for and that 'the keynote of the new system will be that the child is the centre of education' (*ibid.*).

The different types of secondary school must therefore be 'broadly equivalent' (*ibid.*). The White Paper then goes on to outline the now familiar tripartite system, drawing on the Green Book and the Norwood Committee's deliberations. Again, in view of what happened later, it is interesting to read the imaginative aspirations of the authors of the White Paper for the modern schools. Freed of tradition, unlike grammar schools:

> Their future is their own to make, and it is a future full of promise. They offer a general education for life, closely related to interests and environment of the pupils and of a wide range embracing the literary as well as the practical. . . . The further advance of schools of this type depends on a longer school life for the pupils, a more complete reorganisation, better buildings and amenities and a more generous scale of staffing.
>
> (*ibid.*, pp. 9–10)

The White Paper also makes a nod in the direction of the multi-lateral schools lobby:

> Such, then, will be the three main types of secondary schools to be known as grammar, modern and technical schools. It would be wrong to suppose that they will necessarily remain separate and apart. Different types may be combined in one building or on one site. . . . In any case the free interchange of pupils from one type of education to another must be facilitated.
>
> (*ibid.*, p. 10)

After a discussion of the direct-grant schools, the White Paper concludes that a decision on their future should be postponed until the Fleming Committee report. It then makes the all-important promise that all secondary schools 'will be conducted under a single code of regulations', and that fees will be prohibited in all schools for which LEAs are responsible (*ibid.*, p. 11).

The final paragraph of this section mentions the secondary curriculum and refers to the Norwood Committee. Its only recommendation is that:

> consideration must be given to a closer relation of education in the countryside to the needs of agricultural and rural life and, more

generally, to creating a better understanding between the people of the town and of the country.

(*ibid.*)

This was a wartime obsession which had little impact after the war. The acknowledgement in the White Paper that 'laws cannot build better human beings' is, on the other hand, evidence of a welcome humanity which politicians of the present generation would do well to remember.

The next two sections of the White Paper discuss the religious education issues which had absorbed so much of Butler's time over the previous two years. They provide a carefully reasoned account of the compromise that Butler's painstaking negotiations had established. It is argued that:

> Discussions carried on in recent months with the many interests concerned have satisfied the government that there is a wide measure of agreement that voluntary schools should not be abolished but rather that they should be offered further financial assistance, accompanied by a corresponding extension of public control which will ensure the effective and economical organisation and development of both primary and secondary education.
>
> (*ibid.*, p. 14)

In short, they will be permitted to continue but will be subordinated to society's determination to ensure primary and secondary education for all.

The Cowper–Temple compromise is reaffirmed, grants under the 1936 Act for Hadow-style reorganization are promised and then the two options – voluntary-controlled and voluntary-aided – are outlined.

If a school's managers (i.e. governors) are unwilling to meet 50 per cent of the costs of alterations and improvement, they must opt for 'controlled' status, in which case the LEA will take responsibility for appointing and dismissing teachers, subject to the right of the managers to be consulted about the appointment of the headteacher. The managers would also have the right to appoint 'reserved teachers' who could provide denominational instruction for up to two periods a week for those children whose parents desire it. Otherwise, religious education within an agreed syllabus would be required.

The second option – aided status – would be available where the managers were 'able and willing' to meet 50 per cent of the costs of capital repairs and improvements. They would then retain the right to the appointment and dismissal of staff (*ibid.*, p. 16).

In this way, it was argued, existing denominational schools would be enabled to play their part in the reform programme.

The next section of the White Paper concerns itself largely with further and adult education, and the youth service. The most important of its promises in this respect is that 'All young persons from 15 to 18 will be required to attend an appropriate centre part-time unless they are in full-time attendance at school' (*ibid.*, p. 19). Further sections deal with the health and physical well-being of schoolchildren and access to university. Inspection of independent schools is promised, but, as we have seen, all other change in relation to this sector had been postponed pending Fleming's report.

There are two important sections in the latter part of the White Paper, one dealing with the recruitment and training of teachers, and the other with the unit of local educational administration. In 1942 Butler had established a committee of inquiry under Sir Arnold McNair, Vice-Chancellor of Liverpool University. This was not simply a political device as the Fleming Committee was; it was a genuine inquiry into a critical question: how would the rapid expansion of education envisaged in the post-war world be staffed? McNair's report the following year established the framework for teacher training and supply after the war. The White Paper, therefore, confined itself largely to general principles.

> It depends almost entirely upon the quality of those who staff the schools whether the reforms proposed will be merely administrative reforms or whether they will, in practice, work out as real educational reforms.
>
> (*ibid.*, p. 26)

This line of thought was then elucidated:

> if teachers are to meet the needs of children and young persons under the reformed educational system, they must be educated men and women of responsibility whose training has introduced them to a full life which they will be encouraged to maintain, and indeed develop, during their professional careers.
>
> (*ibid.*, p. 27)

Intensive short courses for people currently serving in the forces are promised. Above all, the White Paper argues, 'the task is to present the challenge of the educational service to as wide an audience as possible' in order to attract teachers of 'the calibre to discharge their great responsibilities' (*ibid.*).

With regard to the units of local administration, the White Paper reviews the issues and the options and settles firmly on the proposal that, 'in future the Local Education Authorities shall be the councils of the counties and the county boroughs only'. In other words, Part III authorities were to go. A palliative, however, was offered. The county authorities were 'to prepare schemes for the constitution and functions of district education committees'. These would have a 'general duty of keeping the educational needs of the area under review and making recommendations to the county education committee'. They might also have other responsibilities delegated to them. It was hoped through these means that 'local interest in educational affairs will, therefore, not only be maintained . . . but . . . stimulated and extended over a much wider field' (*ibid.*, p. 30).

MODIFYING THE WHITE PAPER

This has been a lengthy review of a document which itself is only 33 pages long. It bears close scrutiny, not least because it is the seminal educational document of the era. It has a remarkable combination of expansive vision, judicious practicality and authoritative determination. It concluded a period of ferment and consultation. It preceded a year of more detailed consultation and legislation; but the changes made between the White Paper and the Act itself were relatively minor. It would be little exaggeration to claim that *Educational Reconstruction* established the framework for the post-war expansion of education.

A two-day debate in the House of Commons confirmed Butler in his belief that his broad strategy was correct. The immediate response also identified the lines of criticism, on which Butler would spend the autumn working before introducing his Bill. Once the debates on his White Paper in both the Commons and the Lords were out of the way, Butler buckled down to respond to the significant criticisms of his scheme, and to ensure the continued support of the Cabinet for legislation in the forthcoming Parliamentary term.

The most important general criticism was that its timetable for implementation was too leisurely. There were those who argued that the White Paper did not go far enough, or that it lacked radicalism. There were also those, especially among the local authorities, who believed its financial proposals were inadequate. There was further anxiety that the teachers required would simply not be available. It was also felt by many, with some justification, that the White Paper's sections on adult education and the youth service were, in Dent's words, 'brief and vague'. There were those too who suspected – correctly as it turned out – that by leaving the issue of the public schools to the Fleming Committee, the government would avoid reforming them altogether. However, the critics who wanted more, faster, were, from Butler's point of view, allies. They, Butler knew, would not prevent him moving ahead with the Bill. Politically speaking, he had discounted them or rather assumed their support. The ferment in the country would assist him in ensuring that the massed ranks on the Tory back benches would not misbehave.

More dangerous were three other lines of opposition. The Free Churches still had concerns about single-school areas and about the extent of public money being invested in church schools. More threateningly still, the Catholics continued to rage against the whole scheme without proposing any politically credible alternative. Finally, the Association of Education Committees, led by the redoubtable Percival Sharp, wanted a better deal for the Part III authorities. Butler's approach to each of these three lines of opposition are now looked at in turn.

The Free Churches' fears were mollified by Butler through the insertion in the Bill of a clause that required denominational schools to offer not only denominational religious education, but also, if there were parents who wanted it, non-denominational religious education. On the whole, this satisfied the Free Church lobby, which in any case was committed to the overall reform programme. They knew nothing more was on offer.

The Catholics were not so easy to please. Butler now believed that he could proceed regardless of the attitude of the Catholic Church. He had decided that careful political preparation was essential, and that perhaps judicious but minor concessions at crucial moments would help. Meanwhile, Catholic leaders did their best to whip up a popular campaign of opposition. In a statement on the White Paper published in early September, the Catholic hierarchy argued:

> We wish now to make it clear that at no stage have we agreed to the financial conditions now made public. . . . Our people will stand united and determined in what to them is a matter of life and death. They must use every available means to make the justice of their claims widely known and completely understood. We trust that before the Education Bill is tabled and before it is too late to prevent disunity and contention among the people of England and Wales, an equitable arrangement will be sought and reached.
>
> (quoted in *Education*, 3 September 1943)

In this appeal they overestimated their strength in the country – either that or they bluffed. They also underestimated Butler's political skills.

Butler and Ede took the view that the matter of 'life and death' was, behind the rhetoric, a question of money. They also knew that if there was popular pressure it would reach them through those MPs with large Catholic populations in their constituencies. During the third week of September, Butler spent time interviewing MPs individually. They urged him on, even in some cases those under pressure from Catholics. Two Liverpool Labour MPs who represented large numbers of Catholics told him that they were avoiding public meetings in order to keep out of the controversy. A memorandum, drawn up by board officials, on what Catholic schools would gain from the White Paper's proposals was distributed to MPs, and greatly welcomed by them.

In late September Butler reported back to the Lord President's Committee on reactions to the White Paper. He mentioned a Catholic proposal that state loans at low rates of interest should be offered in addition to the existing proposals. The committee, however, saw no reason to make further concessions in addition to what they considered were already generous proposals. The Catholic agitation, therefore, had little effect.

If the agitation had little effect, neither did negotiation. The absence of a recognized leader among the Catholics, and the confusion that resulted, continued to dog relations between them and the government. Cardinal Hinsley, the Archbishop of Liverpool, had died. The leading remaining cleric was Archbishop Downey of Liverpool, who was away in Ireland for much of the year. When the White Paper was debated in the Lords the leading Catholic peers seemed to be ignorant of Butler's discussions with the bishops. Two meetings at Ushaw College in September and October failed to make progress. Butler seemed to have achieved a minor breakthrough with an agreement to establish a joint working party to examine the likely costs of his proposals for the Roman Catholic Church. Downey clearly did not share Butler's view of the discussion. When Butler wrote asking him to name the Catholic representatives Downey replied, restating a fundamentalist position: 'the Catholic claim has always been, and always will be, that the injustice of 1870 and 1876 should be undone' (quoted in Gosden, 1976, p. 320). Later he relented slightly and made a nomination. Inevitably, the Pope had been wheeled in behind the English Catholics. He took the view – with a degree of exaggeration – that the financial pressure the Church was put under, in effect, threatened freedom of conscience.

When the Bill was published there was one sop to the Catholics, though the Church of England benefited too. The 50 per cent grant was extended to cover new schools in cases either where an old school had to be demolished and replaced, or where a general programme of slum clearance was undertaken.

More influential was the campaign by the Association of Education Committees in the proposed new framework. Sir Percival Sharp announced his intentions in his first comment on the White Paper:

> The purely educational proposals of *Educational Reconstruction* are largely, if not entirely, on the lines advocated by the Association of Education Committees. . . . The proposals relating to administration call for immediate comment and examination.
>   If effect be given to the proposals of the White Paper, the autonomy of every Part III Authority, from the largest to the smallest, will be extinguished.
> (*Education*, 23 July 1943, pp. 99–100)

He pointed out that by contrast all LEAs with Part II (i.e. secondary) powers, however small, would retain those powers. In order to maintain the coherence of counties, Mr Butler intends to wipe out the autonomy of 170 Part III authorities. Yet, Sharp continues, 'The importance of the maintenance of local interest and initiative has been stressed at many times by many people – even by Mr Butler himself on more than one occasion.' His plan for doing so in the White Paper, through giving the old Part III authorities the role of reviewing education in their areas and making recommendations to the county, Sharp predicts, 'will prove to be a miserable failure. The surest way of destroying interest is to destroy initiative.' The old Part III authorities

> will not welcome the starveling function with which Mr Butler would clothe them after stripping them bare of the statutory functions they have worn with credit for so long . . . I anticipate that controversy and strong opposition will rage round Mr Butler's areas proposals.

Up to a point Sharp proved to be right. The *Sunday Times* had picked up the AEC line in its first comment on the White Paper. While it saw Butler's proposals as 'administratively unimpeachable', it predicted:

> the smaller boroughs will not accept without a vigorous protest either their dismissal or their mergers in district committees. The fullest use should be made of the efficiency and public spirit which have characterised the education authorities in many of the lesser boroughs.
>
> (*Sunday Times*, 18 July 1943)

After a series of discussions between Butler and the AEC during the autumn, the Bill had shifted from the White Paper what Sir Percival Sharp described as 'a considerable distance' (*Education*, 17 December 1943). There was to be virtual autonomy for a few existing Part III authorities and a much more clearly defined delegation from county authorities to old Part III areas, though the main thrust of the White Paper, the sweeping away of autonomy for many of the smaller old Part III authorities, remained.

Delegated functions included the preparation of a budget to recommend to the county, the supervision of building and repair work (a huge task in the immediate post-war world), the power to recommend the appointment of assistant teachers and consultation with the county authority on the formulation of policy. The district committees would not have the power to borrow money, raise rates or appoint headteachers.

Publicly in 'Week by Week', his regular column in *Education* magazine, Percival Sharp remained unconvinced, but he and his committee welcomed the shift and knew there was no more to be gained. In any case, press and public opinion had never been unanimously behind the AEC's defence of the Part III authorities. *The Times* welcomed Butler's display of flexibility in making concessions, but the *Observer*, *Economist* and *New Statesman* believed he should have stood firm on the White Paper proposals. In the end, the compromise probably owed as much to Chuter Ede as anyone. The respect in which he was held on both sides, and his personal experience at both national and local level in education politics, made him the obvious agent of reconciliation.

THE BILL IN THE COMMONS: 1

The long-awaited Education Bill – described at the time by *Education* as 'the most comprehensive measure in the history of English education' (December 1943) – was given a first reading in the House of Commons on 15 December 1943. The Bill was intended to supersede all previous Education Acts. Broadly speaking, it followed the proposals for Butler's White Paper published five months earlier but, as we have seen, Butler's quest for consensus had led him to make a number of alterations.

In response to pressure from MPs and those keen to see the reform programme forging ahead, the President of the Board of Education was given new powers. In place of his existing responsibility for the 'superintendence of matters relating to education in England and Wales', he was charged with the duty 'to promote the education of the people of England and Wales and the progressive development of institutions devoted to that purpose and to secure the effective execution by local authorities under his control and direction of the national policy'. The Bill also proposed the establishment of two central advisory councils, one for England, one for Wales, to advise the Minister. Unlike the Consultative Committee, which they were to replace, they would not be confined to examining matters referred to them by the Minister. The concessions to the Free Churches and the Catholics referred to in the previous section of this chapter appeared, as did the refined proposals concerning Part III authorities.

The financial provisions made for the Bill's proposals were considerably more generous than those set out in the White Paper. There was a widely welcomed increase in the provision for technical and adult education. Interestingly, in light of the fact that it did not happen until 1973, the financial tables included provision for the raising of the school-leaving age to 16. It was estimated that the total additional cost of the reforms would be £5.5 million in 1946–47, rising gradually to approximately £47 million in 1951–52 and £80 million eventually. There was also provision for the rate of grant paid by central government to local government to be increased from 50 per cent to 55 per cent over a four-year period.

The Bill therefore represented a refinement and an advance on the White Paper. The first reading of any Bill is a formality. The first debate occurs only on the second reading. When this took place, the Christmas holidays were over and the New Year, 1944, had begun. The *Times Educational Supplement* opened the year by wishing its readers:

> A Happy New Year. . . . Everyone hopes, and believes, that 1944 will see the end of the war in Europe and the beginning of a new era in Western Civilisation. . . . There could be no better New Year resolution than to do one's utmost to lay solid foundations for social reconstruction at home and to relieve distress abroad.
>
> (1 January 1944, p. 1)

It then identified in another remarkable editorial the main lines of criticism which Butler could anticipate when the debates on the Bill began in the House of Commons later in the month. The editorial condemns *The Economist*, which had attacked Butler's Bill for ignoring the curriculum: 'From a statutorily imposed curriculum may this country ever be preserved,' it booms. In fact, *The Economist's* case had little support. Other criticisms the editorial anticipated were on inadequate financial provision, the need to strengthen the plans for adult education, and further debate on the structure of local government and the 'religious difficulty'. It concludes:

> On both sides [of the religious controversy] nerves are plainly on edge and it would take little to excite embittered controversy like to that this country has known only too often. That must not be: the times are too grave. . . . It is the plain duty of every man and woman of goodwill to see that the President gets full support in his endeavour to lay a sound foundation for social reconstruction.
>
> (*ibid.*, p. 7)

Butler was clearly only too conscious of the need for calm when, on 19 January, he opened the second reading debate on his Bill. He must also have been proud of the two and a half years of preparation that were now behind him. There were over 250 MPs in the House to hear a 75-minute speech from Butler which was as judicious and statesmanlike as all that he had done since becoming President of the Board of Education.

> I commend to the House a Bill which has been widely welcomed by the many active partners in the world of education. . . . An educational system by itself cannot fashion the whole future structure of a country, but it can make better citizens. 'The principle which our laws have in view,' said Plato, 'is to make the citizens as happy and harmonious as possible.' Such is the modest aim of this Bill, which provides a new framework which will permit of the natural growth and development not only of children, but of national policy itself. This Bill completely recasts the whole of the law as it affects education.
>
> (Hansard, 19 January 1944)

Butler then went on to review his Bill clause by clause. His explanation of the clauses relating to the newly proposed stages of education is a good example of his ability to propose radical change while reassuring the Conservative back benches:

> Let me follow up Clauses 7 and 8 and describe some of the various ways in which this Bill hopes to make our children healthy, happy and worthy of their destiny. Authorities . . . are required to provide nursery schools and classes for children from two to five, before the compulsory age is reached. We do not desire to supplant the home. The family is the healthiest cell of the body politic. But evacuation and war experiences have shown us that many homes need helping, and that family life is buttressed by nursery schools, for which our country seems to have a special bent. They are very often centres of education for the parents themselves. We hope to see the primary schools with smaller classes, and the present fine senior modern schools developing within the secondary sphere in their own way, perhaps with special rural or technical sides.
>
> (*ibid.*)

Promoting the Bill's clauses relating to compulsory part-time education for 15- to 18-year-olds and to the raising of the school-leaving age, Butler rejected the traditional criticism of some employers:

> To the question, 'Who will do the work if everyone is educated?', we reply that education itself will oil the wheels of industry and will bring a new efficiency – the fruit of modern knowledge to the ancient skill of farm and field.
>
> (*ibid.*)

He goes on to reassure those critics, Ernest Bevin among them, who were anxious that a school-leaving age of 16 would be endlessly postponed.

What is the government's policy about raising the age to 16? The educational reasons for raising the age to 16 are conclusive. The only hesitation to naming a definite date derives from the need to press ahead with reorganisation and other educational reforms. . . . I mention specifically reduction in the size of classes and provision of more teachers and suitable buildings. In planning future secondary schools of all types, authorities should have in mind that 16 will eventually be the normal leaving age.

(ibid.)

Butler then reviewed his plans for providing teachers and buildings and moved on to discuss post-15 education in more depth. Turning to direct-grant schools, he once again reassured Conservatives while trying to cajole those who wanted fees to be abolished in these schools:

A heavy-handed insistence on the prohibition of fees in all direct grant schools would be likely to result in the governors of some such schools deciding to leave the State system. . . . Such a step would have an effect diametrically opposite to what the opponents of fees in direct grant schools desire, since it would inevitably accentuate social distinctions and widen the gap between the schools.

(ibid.)

Butler's analysis proved broadly accurate, as Shirley Williams discovered when she pressed ahead with the abolition of direct-grant schools in the late 1970s. He then moved on to the most sensitive area of all: the Dual System. Explaining with care the compromise brought about by his negotiations, he was gentle but firm.

there is no disputing the general proposition that the years from 1902 onwards have shown a progressive inability on the part of managers of voluntary schools to discharge their statutory liabilities.

(ibid.)

The White Paper had sufficiently explained the problem, he said. His Bill was designed to solve it by bringing 'the Church schools along in as close a partnership as possible, eliminating as much of the friction involved in the operation of the Dual system as we can. . . . The proposals which I have outlined have received a wide measure of support in the course of full and frank discussion with bodies and persons holding widely differing views, and I suggest to the House they should not be lightly dismissed'. This was a beautifully understated expression of a heartfelt sentiment. He followed it with a threat aimed at the Catholic hierarchy:

> Any alternative which does not take account of the traditional policy that any further increased public aid must be accompanied by increased public control would, I am convinced, imperil its general acceptance, and might bring about a reaction as detrimental to the Churches as to the cause of education itself.
>
> (*ibid.*)

As for the financial deal he was offering:

> The new terms are generous and we are ready to have them fully examined and discussed. In return I think I can at least ask those who feel deeply on these matters to dismiss from their minds the wholly unwarrantable view that the Government desires either to tear away Church schools from unwilling managers or to force them inhumanely out of business.
>
> (*ibid.*)

He then turned to the improved financial arrangements for implementing the whole of the Bill, making the point that there would be a 'proper discrimination' in favour of poor authorities. He pointed out that while he could see the case for a complete overhaul of local government and its finance, he would not wish to hold up his reforms until that unspecified moment in the future. In the mean time, he urged local authorities to show 'zeal and foresight' in implementing the Bill. He concluded in words which deserve to be recorded in full:

> The House will realize that the scope of the Bill is very wide indeed. Yet there are aspects of it which I have not yet described. There are some who are anxious about the burden which the Bill may impose. But there are few who have not commented favourably on the substance and range of the measure. Perhaps this Bill owes its welcome to an appreciation of the synthesis which it tries to create between order and liberty, between the voluntary agency and the state, between the private life of a school and the public life of its district, between manual and intellectual skill, and between those better and those less well-endowed.
>
> But more than that. As the reforms this Bill provides for are made effective, we shall develop as never before our most abiding assets, our richest resources – the character and competence of a great people; and, as I believe, in a manner not unworthy of our people's greatness.
>
> (*ibid.*)

In short, his Bill was one designed to unite a people who would – with their allies – within the foreseeable future ensure the defeat of Fascism in Europe.

Butler himself was justly proud of his second reading speech, and devoted two pages of his autobiography to it. He clearly enjoyed the drama of it, particularly the section on the Dual System.

> I had just got to the part in my speech in which I anticipated playing against the wind when Mgr Griffin, the newly appointed Archbishop of Westminster . . . was ushered into the Distinguished Strangers' Gallery. There, with the sun illuminating his bright red hair and his pectoral cross, he sat looking directly down on me as I outlined the provisions of the religious settlement and replied to those who had criticized its compromises [arguing that] . . . 'The best way I can reassure them is by quoting a verse from a hymn:
>
> > "Ye fearful saints fresh courage take
> > The clouds ye so much dread
> > Are big with mercy and shall break
> > In blessings on your head" '
>
> The unexpected, gratifying and witty sequel was the delivery to me next morning of a large parcel, containing not a bomb, but a set of Abbot Butler's *Lives of the Saints*, the classic Roman Catholic work on hagiography.
>
> (Butler, 1971, pp. 118–19)

Butler's cheerful anecdote records the moment when, symbolically at least, the Catholic Church accepted defeat. Certainly the debates in Parliament were far less traumatic and vitriolic than many had feared. The Labour MP for Romford, Mr Parker, followed Butler and promised that his party would back the Minister in his efforts to get the measure through the House. The Labour party would assist in any struggle against vested interests or the forces of snobbery. He was critical of two aspects of the Bill: its failure to deal with the 'so-called public schools', and the lack of a definite date for the raising of the school-leaving age to 16. He shared the widespread concern about recruiting sufficient teachers and indicated that if a choice had to be made between the development of young people's college for 15- to 18-year-olds and preparations for raising the leaving age to 16, his party would prefer to see the latter.

A succession of further speakers followed, many of them congratulatory in tone. The Conservative MP for Norwich, Sir Geoffrey Shakespeare, was more eloquent in his praise than most. Butler had produced a Bill which 'gathers up the dreams of all education reformists and is the first Bill which I remember that deals with the whole of the educable life of the child' (Hansard, 19 January 1944).

Butler must have been reassured by the contributions in the debate on the religious issue. Shakespeare pressed Butler on the single-school areas, which he said were 'a national disgrace', but made clear his support for the Bill. From the Catholic angle, Sir Patrick Hannon, also a Conservative, complimented Butler's patience and diplomacy but wished further consideration would be given to the financial aspects of Butler's proposals on the Dual System. He assured the House that Catholic feeling supported the Bill and said he would support the second reading. He hoped, however, that in the committee stage, 'something would be done to remove the suspicion in Catholic minds that they were being treated differently and on a lower footing than others' (*ibid.*).

The debate went on to raise the other issues Butler had expected: direct-grant schools, the school-leaving age, finance, teacher supply, buildings, and local administration. So often in these cases, ministers find themselves listening to speeches from backbenchers which seem stale and outdated. They, after all, have been living and breathing the issues; for the backbenchers, on the other hand, it is often a first opportunity to participate in a great debate and to put on record, for their constituents and history, their views, however often the Minister may have heard such views before.

The second day of the debate was opened by Arthur Greenwood, who, since Attlee and other leading Labour MPs were ministers, had been Leader of the Opposition since February 1942. Greenwood was a Labour heavyweight who would have been more influential still had he not suffered from a drink problem. Butler would have listened with care to his speech.

Certainly his case for tightening up the timetable and bringing forward a school-leaving age of 16 made an impact on Harold Dent. On 29 January, in his editorial, he quoted with approval Greenwood's cry that 'unless we deal with this problem of education, this war against ignorance, with the same intensity as we have dealt with the war against Hitler, we shall not get for the rising generation the kind of education that they deserve' (*TES*, 29 January 1944, p. 55).

This is a typical piece of wartime demagogy of the type associated with the New Jerusalemers. It undoubtedly had its effect at the time. Chuter Ede, the Parliamentary Secretary, wound up the debate and spent the greater part of his time on the religious issue. He turned also to the financing of poorer local authorities, presumably with the aim of reassuring his Labour colleagues in particular.

> We expect to be compelled to come to the House . . . with some scheme . . . [to] make the burden of those districts which have a high child population and a low rateable value less heavy than it is at the present time.
>
> (Hansard, 20 January 1944)

After demonstrating a reassuring grasp of the problem of teacher recruitment, he concluded with a flourish. The government was presenting to the House the first comprehensive education measure ever. Fisher's Act had not tackled either of the most intractable issues, the Dual System or the local authorities.

> We have for good or ill attempted to survey the whole field, educational, administrative and religious, and we believe that our measure is such that we shall be able, when it gets on the statute-book, to proceed with diligence in our endeavour to make this Act of Parliament a living reality.
>
> (*ibid.*)

The Bill was read a second time, without need for a division.

In the country, evidence of support came from all sides. On the first day of the second reading debate, a letter appeared in *The Times* from ten leading industrialists announcing that:

> We as industrialists desire to support the Government's proposals for educational reform. We welcome the raising of the school leaving-age to 15 and subsequently to 16, the provision of part-time education for those between the ages of 15 and 18, and the extension of technical and adult education.
>
> These reforms may be said to involve a financial burden on industry: we should accept that burden gladly, because we believe that industry will thereby gain in efficiency and the country in well-being.
>
> (*The Times*, 19 January 1944)

A week later, the British Council of Churches held a meeting at Friends' House in the Euston Road in support of the Bill. William Temple, the Archbishop of Canterbury, welcomed the Bill as 'a notable contribution to social justice, to fuller national fellowship and to growth in religious knowledge' (*TES*, 29 January 1944, p. 54).

On 27 January, even the Conservative sub-committee, whose reactionary views had been a constant source of embarrassment to Butler, urged support for the Bill, though they expressed concerns about its cost: 'the Sub-Committee insists on the need for realism as well as enthusiasm' (*ibid.*).

Typical of hundreds of meetings held around that time was one in Kirkby Stephen on 29 January. Organized jointly by the Westmorland (East Ward) National Union of Teachers Association and the local WEA, the main speaker was a recently retired HMI and the chair a former headmistress of the local grammar school. The *TES* report concludes: 'A resolution was passed welcoming the Bill and hoping that its main features would be implemented' (*TES*, 5 February 1944, p. 68).

On 28 January the Bill's financial resolution, drawn in broad terms so as not to restrict debate in the committee stage, was agreed. The Bill then proceeded to committee. Butler had proposed to the Chief Whip, James Stuart, that Part II of the Bill, which included the Dual System, should be dealt with in an ordinary Committee and the rest of the Bill in the whole House sitting as a committee. He felt that a wrangle over religion in the whole House would be 'undignified' in wartime. Stuart rejected this suggestion and recommended that the whole committee stage should be in the whole House since an ordinary committee 'could more easily not do the behest of the government' (Gosden, 1976, p. 321). Butler conceded, and the committee stage did indeed take place in the whole House, enabling any MP who so wished to participate.

THE BILL IN THE COMMONS: 2

After two days of the committee stage, only six of the 111 clauses had been debated, and clear-cut decisions had been reached on only three. The *TES* editorial counselled those who, out in the country, were becoming impatient: 'There are times for speed and times for hastening slowly. The Committee stage of a great measure of social reform is among the latter' (*TES*, 12 February 1944, p. 78). This was particularly the case, it argued, when the major committee debate had been on a fundamental issue: the balance of power between central and local government. An amendment to restrict the power of the Minister had been defeated. Messer's amendment which proposed to change the title of 'President of the Board of Education' to 'Minister of Education' found widespread support, especially from Sir Thomas Moore (Ayr Burghs), who apparently provoked loud laughter by saying that the old title gave the impression of a benign chairman presiding over a gaggle of wise old owls (*ibid.*). Greenwood announced that the opposition felt sufficiently strongly to take the issue to a division. Butler promised to look at it again, and the amendment was withdrawn. In the later draft of the Bill, the old title was indeed swept away and replaced by the word 'Minister'. Since there had not been a board to be president of for many years, this seemed to make sense.

In spite of the calming advice of the *TES* editorial, Butler himself became concerned at the slowness of the Bill's progress. By the middle of February, the committee had only reached Clause 14. Partly, as the *TES* had suggested, this was a result of the significance of the measure. Partly, too, it was a result of MPs glad to have something to get their teeth into in a wartime Parliament short of business. As Arthur Greenwood remarked tetchily in the debate of 28 March, 'I am bound to say that I have known few Bills on which so many Second Reading speeches have been made during the Committee stage as this' (Hansard, 28 March 1944).

Butler took up his concern with James Stuart. 'It could not but do the government great harm if it appeared that the Bill might not make enough progress to give an earnest of the government's intentions,' he wrote (rather clumsily). After discussing the problem with Stuart, Butler decided to call a meeting of the most active MPs in the debate (Gosden, 1976, p. 321). He ensured that all those MPs who were spokespeople for the major interests were included. Following the meeting in early March there was a general effort to expedite the passage of the Bill, but there were several major issues still to be debated later in March, one of which almost upset the entire applecart.

Meanwhile, outside the Commons, Butler, following up his second reading commitment, continued discussions with the churches on their financial concerns. Eventually he conceded a scheme of loans to put the church authorities on a par with local authorities. This solved one problem the churches had faced. The banks had previously refused to make loans to them on the grounds that the trusts which governed the church schools prevented the use of their buildings for non-educational purposes; they were therefore not acceptable to the banks as security.

On 20 April 1944 the new Archbishop, Mgr Griffin, grudgingly accepted the arrangement: 'We have not received justice, nor have our claims been met, but if you study the amended Bill, you will find that the Board has gone a considerable way to meet many of our representations' (quoted in Gosden, 1976, p. 322). This was hardly an example of Christian generosity, but it was enough.

Meanwhile, after further discussions in the Lord President's Committee, Butler had also increased the financial provision for the poorest local authorities from £900,000 to over £1.5 million. Neither these financial concessions nor Butler's meeting with the leading MPs was sufficient to ensure that the committee kept to the timetable the government had mapped out. Indeed, in the last ten days of March the committee became decidedly restive and the government found itself in difficulty.

The first serious problem arose on Clause 23, when Mrs Thelma Cazalet Keir, Conservative MP for Islington East and one of a group of active Tory reformers, moved that the school-leaving age should be raised to 16 within three years of Part II of the Act coming into force. Butler had always been sympathetic to those who wanted a school-leaving age of 16; indeed he had said as much in the second reading debate. He was mindful, however, both of over-committing the government's resources and of frightening cautious cabinet colleagues. In any case, he believed genuinely that local authorities would have their work cut out to repair war damage and achieve a school-leaving age of 15. It was an issue where he knew his own assessment of *realpolitik* was out of kilter with the aspirations of the general public, of many MPs and even of some ministers.

Using argumentation more usually heard on the Labour benches, Mrs Cazalet Keir put her case:

> There is no need to argue this amendment on educational grounds. It is admitted in the Bill, and universally accepted. All parents who can afford it do, in fact, keep their children at school full time until 16 and even later.
>
> (Hansard, 21 March 1944)

Tackling the administrative arguments, she asserted: 'I am sure that local education authorities would prefer a definite time rather than some shadowy date'. Butler had, after all, said they must take account in their plans of a leaving age of 16. Without a definite date, 'there will always be good reasons given for postponement, and none of us wants to see another demi-semi-implemented Fisher Act on the Statute Book'.

Moelwyn Hughes, MP for Carmarthen, seconded Cazalet Keir's amendment and reminded the House that if the decision was left to the Minister, in practice it would be a decision for the whole government. Could a government be relied on? He raised the spectre of the wasted decades which had just passed.

> We may find a Geddes or a May Committee and a Government ready to hand over to them the right to over-ride what Parliament, a little while before, had decided was desirable; to over-ride even what the President of the Board agreed was the right thing to do by education.

This was powerful stuff. The argument against a specified date was taken up by another Welshman, Professor Gruffydd, who represented the University of Wales. He accepted the sentiment of the movers, but 'it is quite impossible to raise the school-leaving age to 16, within any time it would be profitable to mention . . . in a Bill . . . [The President of the Board] is as powerless as the meanest Member of the farthest Back Bench to modify the present policy of the Minister of Labour towards teachers'.

Mrs Cazalet Keir interrupted to ask if in that case he was also opposed to specifying the date for a school-leaving age of 15.

'Yes,' he replied, 'I am against it. The teachers necessary for all the boys and girls between 14 and 16 are simply not in existence . . . . A vast number of them, as a matter of fact, are now engaged in peeling potatoes and cleaning lavatories in the Services'.

His basic argument was that 'a decent occupation where the problems of adolescence would have . . . at least a partial solution' would be preferable to being compelled to go to an inadequately staffed school. Further passion was brought to bear in the argument by Nancy Astor, Britain's first woman MP and, by 1944, something of a veteran, and from W. G. Cove, Labour MP for Aberavon, a radical former miner who had later been President of the NUT.

Lady Astor began assertively:

> I mean business when it comes to raising of the school age. I am not one of those people who believe that education is popular. I do not agree with [Professor Gruffydd] that this [amendment] is a political stunt and that it is popular . . . . If it had been popular we should have had the Fisher Act, which was one of the best Acts in the world. We did not get it because it was not popular with any party.

Sir Herbert Williams, the Conservative who represented Croydon South interrupted: 'May I ask the noble lady a question?'

'I do not want to talk to the Hon. Member either in the House or outside,' she replied. Sir Herbert, taken aback, reminded her that on the last occasion they had spoken she had asked him a favour. 'If she cannot learn good manners, it is not my fault.'

'I apologise to the Hon. Member, but I have . . . seen that he is one of the most diehard Tories the world has ever seen,' replied Lady Astor.

At this point the chair intervened, but the debate had reached a new intensity. Nancy Astor returned to her theme:

> We talk about the future of democracy being in the hands of youth – but not an uneducated youth . . . the Government should make this a question of real national push . . . I do not want to say a word against the Minister of Education. He has been absolutely magnificent.

There were no votes to be gained during the debates on the Bill in attacking Butler personally, since his statesmanlike qualities were recognized on all sides. Lady Astor continued:

> but I do not believe . . . the Cabinet have been magnificent. . . . What is the Minister of Reconstruction going to reconstruct if all the young people are turned out at 15 – and this after all the tosh that is being talked about youth?

Lady Astor concluded in typical wartime style with a side-swipe at Fascism and a plea to pull together:

> Our education teaches people not what to think but how to think. We shall have to think hard if this country is to keep its place in the future. We must be willing to face things that seem difficult in the future, in the same way we face war problems and with the same courage.

W. G. Cove, following her, reminded the House that he had started to work in the pit at the age of 12.

> I want . . . to give the children of the working class a chance of free development. . . . Hon. Members opposite [the Conservatives] intelligently and elementarily give that chance to their children and what the best parent wants for his child society should want for all.

As for buildings and teachers:

> I am not on the side of the planners. I am on the side of the improvisers. We have improvised for evacuation and we have done

miracles in evacuation. We have accomplished the impossible in evacuation . . . why not apply the same temper, tone, will and power to the post-war period? . . . You cannot have democracy unless you get this raising of the school leaving age to 16 . . . this Bill as far as equality of opportunity is concerned is a farce unless the school leaving age is raised to 16 or there is a definite promise to this effect.

Cove concluded his impassioned, perhaps excessively aggressive, contribution by arguing that Butler had found money to achieve compromise with the churches but not to achieve a school-leaving age of 16. A case such as that would have brought cheers at a Labour party or NUT meeting; it was not likely to bring doubtful Tory backbenchers into the lobbies with him.

Before Butler attempted to answer his critics, Sir Herbert Williams, thoroughly riled, rose to defend the government's position. Butler must have wished he had stayed in his seat. Williams began by attacking Cove: 'I am a little disappointed that those who are so enthusiastic about education should show such an incredible capacity for being irrelevant.' He then ran through some practical arguments before reaching the crux of his diehard case: 'Anyone who is a truthful realist knows that the raising of the school leaving age above 14 will be a most incredible waste of the time of great masses of children.' Sacrifice on behalf of children was part of the meaning of education, he argued, and he objected to an amendment that implied that 'we must all spend the same amount on cultural things like education'. He was interrupted by Quintin Hogg, the youthful liberal Conservative MP for Oxford who later became Lord Chancellor under Margaret Thatcher, and by a Labour MP who accused him of talking 'a lot of twaddle', but he had already made his substantive point.

Butler summed up his case calmly, putting before the committee 'some idea of the heavy responsibilities which lie on our shoulders in deciding what the future priorities of education reform are to be'. He emphasized the practicalities: 'I am advised that another 406,000 [school] places are necessary to raise the age to 16. . . . As it is, we have to find 391,000 extra school places to raise the age to 15.'

He listed the array of tasks facing him once the Bill was passed, mentioning among them 'the question of limiting the size of classes to 30 . . . one of the most important reforms of all'. He also pointed out the confusion the amendment would cause for those planning young persons' colleges for 15- to 18-year-olds. As a concession, he made a commitment that 'the Minister shall undertake annually to report to Parliament on the progress of reorganisation and on the number of teachers which shall be available for carrying out the raising of the age to 16'.

Arthur Greenwood then declared the Labour party's support for the amendment and intention to divide the House on it. It is worth noting that the post-war Labour government failed to achieve the school-leaving age of 16, and indeed came close to delaying the implementation of the age of 15; the post-war realities overwhelmed their undoubted wartime idealism precisely as Butler had predicted.

When the vote came, the government won by 172 votes to 137, a majority of 35. This, by wartime standards, was a close-run thing. Twenty-five Tories had voted with the Labour Party, including Thelma Cazalet Keir, Quintin Hogg and Peter Thorneycroft. It was clear enough evidence that the committee was becoming, from a government point of view, ill-disciplined. The *Times Educational Supplement* on the following Saturday took a strongly pro-Butler line. Those who had voted against the government had demonstrated a 'depressing' lack of trust in government. True, it accepted, the 1920s and 1930s gave cause for lack of trust, but surely 'our political affairs will be conducted on a higher plane in the future'. The *TES*, therefore, backed Butler's realism and said it was 'up to Parliament and the public as well as the Minister to see that "as soon as practicable" means as soon as practicable' (25 March 1944, p. 151). There is an irony here. The *TES* case for realism was based on a disarming, widely shared but naïve idealism that post-war politics would be conducted quite differently from the politics of the past.

It was the following Tuesday, 28 March, that the government was actually defeated, for the only time on any issue during the war. Though Butler might have sensed the committee's restlessness, he could hardly have predicted the issue on which he faced defeat.

The predictable debate on direct-grant schools was the first major issue of the day. It drew out the predictable arguments from predictable participants. The result, too, was predictable: a comfortable government majority. Further amendments came and went before Mrs Cazalet Keir, for the second time in eight days, moved an amendment that put Butler under pressure. Into a clause referring to the teachers' pay negotiating body, the Burnham Committee, she proposed to insert a phrase which would prevent differentiation of pay on grounds of sex. Up to that point it had been generally accepted that men should be paid roughly 20 per cent more than women for the same work.

There had been general discussions in the House before on the issue of equal pay, particularly with regard to the Civil Service, but this was an Education Bill so Mrs Cazalet Keir chose to argue the case not on general grounds, but specifically in relation to teachers. The case, she claimed, was clear-cut:

> Men and women enter the same training colleges at the same age, with the same entrance qualifications. They take equivalent courses of training for exactly the same length of time: when they emerge from the training colleges, they receive the same certificates from the Board of Education or the University and they enter their professional lives in exactly the same way by applying for teaching posts when vacancies occur. When they get into schools they are confronted by the same problems, responsibilities and conditions of work.
>
> (Hansard, 28 March 1944)

It was a brief but effective speech. Major Peter Thorneycroft, later Chairman of the Conservative Party in the early Thatcher era, but then a young Tory reformer, seconded the amendment. 'I am not a feminist,' he asserted, '. . . but I firmly hold the view that . . . the job should go to the most efficient person, whether man or woman, and that payment should be based on that principle.' He foresaw that he and his colleagues would be told that they could not deal with teachers separately from the Civil Service.

> I know that the path of a reformer, may I say even a Tory reformer, is a hard one . . . I believe if [the President of the Board] accepts my hon. friend's amendment not only will it be a great social reform, but it will also be better attuned to that sense of social justice which is commonly held today.

Dr Haden Guest, a Labour MP, followed Thorneycroft: 'I am very glad indeed to hear the speech which has just been made, the first pink dawn of a red awakening'.

The sixth speaker in the debate was the famous Glaswegian radical, Jimmy Maxton, who argued that MPs were paid at equal rates – man or woman – and that the same should apply to teachers. Furthermore, he argued, on the whole women teachers were more successful. Nancy Astor, following him, agreed and continued:

> If this were the last vote I ever gave in my life, I would give it in favour of this Amendment, because I have watched teachers pressing for equal pay for 24 years and I have seen the prejudice with which they have been met.

Butler was next, the eighth speaker and yet the first to oppose the amendment. He must have been concerned that he was facing defeat even then. He was also acutely embarrassed because he would find himself depending on the backwoods Tories he so despised to defeat the liberal Tories and Labour members who had, on the whole, given his project staunch support. The last thing he wanted to do was to see a political edge entering the debates on the Bill, from which they had been remarkably absent: 'We have not had any such atmosphere in Committee on the Bill and I do not propose that education should be used as a stalking-horse for people's political views.'

He wanted instead to be 'business-like'. The committee should recognize that it was the local authorities which employed teachers and that it had not been 'usual . . . for the Minister to give directions to the Burnham panels'. Burnham could, if it wished, raise the question itself, whereas the proposed amendment 'destroys a form of machinery on which we have depended for the teachers' contentment for a very long time'.

He then pointed out that it was indeed a wider issue than one for teachers on which the Chancellor of the Exchequer would have a view. He was prepared to discuss the issue with him, 'armed with the arguments that have been put forward today . . . but to request me to put in this provision before the general question is decided would be wrong for the reasons I have given'. He warned 'reformers, whether they be Tory reformers or others', that 'a division against the government is not just a demonstration, it is a serious thing'. Worse still, 'by mobilising forces and voting against me, I can only say that I do not think it is in the interest of this great reform which I hold in my hand'. Not once did he enter into the actual issue of equal pay; instead he hoped to win over the young Tory reformers with this appeal to loyalty.

Four further speakers supported the amendment, before some feeble support for Butler came from Mr T. Mangay, MP for Gateshead, who simply claimed that among all the representations he had received in his constituency, not one had supported equal pay.

Quintin Hogg (later Lord Hailsham) entered the fray, powerfully on the side of Cazalet Keir. He began by sympathizing with Butler's predicament and complimenting him on his courage, but:

> It seems to me a little unjust to suggest that because, as we know, he is a great reformer and a sincere believer in reform, we should be bound to take his advice on every occasion, or if not on every occasion, at least not to disregard it more than once a week.

Butler was wrong to argue that the amendment would overturn the Burnham machinery; it was rather 'laying down once and for all . . . the guiding principle which should govern the working of the Burnham machinery'.

As for Butler's point that decisions on equal pay for teachers could not be made in isolation from the Civil Service, Hogg sympathized, but took the view that Parliamentary time was precious and reformers had to take the opportunities that arose to determine the principle. In any case, they had no evidence that 'if we do not press this matter to a Division now we shall get a debate on equal pay for civil servants within a reasonable time'.

Ivor Thomas, MP for Keighley, and then Butler intervened. Was Hogg saying that if there was a guarantee of a debate on equal pay in the Civil Service before Easter, the amendment would be withdrawn?

Hogg came under some pressure. Though he and his friends had a motion on the Order Paper favouring equal pay for civil servants, they had not pressed for debate before Easter. Hogg tried to argue that the task of urging a debate at a specific time was the responsibility of those who had put their names to the amendment. His was not one of them.

Butler intervened again to taunt him.

> Is it not the fact that the Hon. Member has such control over his followers that he must be responsible for everything they do? I understand that the discipline among his followers is of a very high standard.

Hogg, somewhat diverted from his theme, concluded by urging that passing the amendment was the most appropriate way of progressing the issue.

Flight-Lieutenant Raikes, Conservative MP for Essex South East, then rose to say a word or two in support of the Minister, and accused Hogg of having been 'rather tiresomely virtuous'. The Minister was right to try to avoid interfering with Burnham. Edith Summerskill argued that without the equal pay clause the Bill would 'be a measure of reform but not a great measure'. If the women doctors who worked in schools were paid the same as men, why not the women teachers?

William Gallacher, the fiery Labour MP for Fife West, brought a new angle to the debate. Enjoying himself hugely, he mocked the young Tories for seizing 'upon some particularly feasible proposal and [using] it for unscrupulous demagogy'. The real basis for equal pay could be found in Marx: 'I'm arguing the case for equal opportunity, or payment according to worth, the young Tories are arguing for something very desirable – the elimination of themselves and their class – for they are worth nothing'. It was the Labour movement alone that was responsible for real progress: 'If Providence has no other means of giving effect to its desire than through the young Tories, then Providence must be in a very sad way'.

This was a witty attack on Butler's tormentors, but it offered him no comfort. Commander Sir Archibald Southby, Conservative MP for Epsom, who might have been expected to help, simply made things worse. Butler had offered nothing except that he would make representations to the Chancellor, yet the House wanted a decision on an issue of principle. W. A. Colgate, the last backbench speaker, came to his aid: 'to bring this in at the tag end of a clause . . . seems to me a great mistake and for that reason I shall certainly vote for the government'. Butler came in again in a last-ditch attempt to stave off defeat, but could offer nothing more than disarming honesty:

> The only thing which remains for me to say is that if people do not like the way I have expressed my case I am very sorry. I have been put in a difficult position and it would be much worse for me to undertake to do what I know I cannot conscientiously carry out and therefore I must put myself and the Government in the hands of the Committee.

When the votes were counted, the government had lost by 117 to 116, with 37 Conservatives in the majority. The result surprised those on the government bench. Tory reformers were shocked too. Butler himself recalls showing a measure of irritation at the result. He also remembered that 'we should have escaped defeat, if only one of the less sprightly Ministers, like Sir John Anderson, who had been working in their offices in Whitehall, had proved more fleet of foot' (Butler, 1971, p. 120). A rather confused procedural discussion followed. Those who had voted for the amendment were at pains to make clear, as Greenwood put it, that 'this vote is not a vote of lack of confidence in my Right Hon. friend the President of the Board of Education'.

Anthony Eden, Foreign Secretary and Leader of the House, refused to give any undertaking 'of any sort. . . . What we shall do, is to consider the result of this vote and make our view upon it plain at the earliest possible moment'. He meant that the Prime Minister would have to be consulted. Butler apparently slammed his documents into his dispatch case and walked out (Howard, 1987, p. 137). Meanwhile, with the excitement over, and the House of Commons virtually empty, a handful of MPs went on to hear the adjournment debate on the fascinating topic of, in *Hansard*'s words, 'CAMP SITE, WELSH COAST' (Hansard, 28 March 1944).

Two days earlier, on Sunday, 26 March, Winston Churchill had made one of his broadcast addresses, which were listened to avidly across the country. By March 1944 the war was moving the Allies' way, and Churchill was increasingly prepared to accept the views of those, like Butler, who advised him to take account of the ferment of interest in rebuilding British society after the war. In his broadcast he referred to plans 'to make our island home a better place after the war', including 'a reform and an advance on a great scale of the education of the people'. He went on:

> I may draw your attention to the fact that several of these large measures, which a year ago I told you might be accomplished after the war was over, have already been shaped and framed and presented to Parliament and the public. For instance, you have the greatest scheme of improved education that has ever been attempted by a responsible government. This will soon be on the Statute Book.
> (quoted in *Education*, 31 March 1944, p. 382)

Churchill was a deeply tired man. The preparations for the Normandy landings were taking their toll, and there was growing anxiety over Germany's development of a rocket bomb. The main purpose of his broadcast had been to prepare the British people to face the new perils ahead.

> Britain can take it. She has never flinched or failed. And when the signal is given, the whole circle of avenging nations will hurl themselves upon the foe and batter the life out of the cruellest tyranny which has ever sought to bar the progress of mankind.
>
> (quoted in Gilbert, 1991, p. 770)

On the day of the government defeat, General Brook, Chief of the Imperial General Staff, noted of Churchill in his diary:

> We found him in desperately tired mood. I am afraid that he is losing ground rapidly. He seems quite incapable of concentrating for a few minutes on end and keeps wandering continuously.
>
> (quoted *ibid.*)

In short, when the exhausted Prime Minister heard of the government's defeat in Parliament, he had other overwhelmingly more important matters on his mind than what to him must have seemed the petty manoeuvrings of a bunch of disloyal young Tories. It was also embarrassing to see such turmoil on the very Bill he had referred to in his broadcast. No wonder then that he behaved in a way that to some seemed petulant, 'cracking a nut with a sledge-hammer', as Colville called it (*ibid.*, p. 771). He insisted on a vote of confidence. According to *Education* (31 March 1944, p. 383), it was reported that Butler had tendered his resignation, but Butler's own version of events refutes this suggestion. Churchill's chief concern was to humble the rebel Tories and make clear to the world that the government had the full confidence of the House of Commons. Harold Nicholson tried to persuade him to find a milder method of dealing with them, but the Prime Minister appears to have been personally offended by the vote. He told Nicholson, 'I am not going to tumble round my cage like a wounded canary. You knocked me off my perch. You have now got to put me back on my perch. Otherwise I won't sing' (Nicholson's diary, quoted in Gilbert, 1991, p. 771).

According to Butler, he was asked to go with the Chief Whip to see Churchill at about a quarter to ten.

> We found Churchill in a very resolute and jovial mood. He said that he warmly supported my language, which he had heard on the nine o'clock news; he was sorry that the issue should have been that of equal pay, but it was not the issue that mattered so much as the opportunity to rub the rebels' noses in their mess. He had long been waiting for this opportunity; the by-elections had been going against him, and the House seemed to be utterly unaware that there was a war on and that we had severe struggles ahead. Now the Lord had delivered the enemy into his hands.
>
> (Butler, 1971, p. 121)

Hence his firm statement to the House on the day after the debate:

> The event of yesterday requires an alteration in government business. It would not be possible for His Majesty's Government to leave matters where they stood. . . . At this very time in the progress of the war, there must be no doubt or question of the support which the Government enjoys in the House of Commons. Accordingly, we have decided . . . to resume the Committee stage of the Education Bill and to delete Clause 82, as amended, entirely from the Measure. This act of deletion will be regarded as a Vote of Confidence in the present Administration. If the Government does not secure an adequate majority, it will entail the usual consequences [i.e. the resignation of the government and a General Election]. Should the House agree to the deletion of the Clause, the Government proposes to move to reinstate the original Clause, without the Amendment, on the Report stage, and to treat its passage throughout as a matter of confidence.
>
> (Hansard, 29 March 1944)

Churchill achieved his objectives. The government won a huge majority – approaching 400 – in the confidence vote and the hapless rebels were humiliated. The Prime Minister was in his element dealing with them in the House. When Mrs Cazalet Keir asked him what point there was in a committee stage if the government was going to treat all amendments like this, he replied, drily:

> I hesitate to make declarations about the future. . . . But I should not hesitate in hazarding the suggestion that every Amendment must be judged on its merits and in the relation which it has to the general policy of the Government.

The rebels, meanwhile, made bemused speeches. Quintin Hogg, their upstart leader, had the excess of confidence which enabled him to say, 'I was hoping that the Prime Minister was in the process of yielding to my persuasion'. Some hope. He also referred to their 'embarrassment'.

Of course they had no choice but to support the government, but some of them complained that treating any defeat in a committee as a matter of confidence inhibited the Parliamentary process. Churchill explained that this was not the case.

> The Government have accepted, I am told, 50 or 60 amendments. The whole Bill is being shaped as it goes along. The reason that this difficulty arose was that something much bigger and extraneous was tacked on.

Of course, the Labour Party, which was integrally involved in the coalition government, and indeed perhaps the dominant influence on the home front, had no intention of voting against the government either. On the whole, though, Labour MPs enjoyed the confusion the whole affair created among the Tories.

There was no such pleasure at the débâcle in educational circles. Shortly after the government defeat, the NUT President, Ronald Gould, met the General Secretary, Frederick Mander, to discuss what should be done. Gould believed that 'the fate of the Bill hung in the balance' (Gould, 1976, p. 105). In spite of the NUT's policy commitment to equal pay, he and Mander took the view that the priority should be to 'save the Bill at all costs'. They contacted all NUT members in the House and any other friendly MPs to make this clear (*ibid.*).

Education, the journal of the Association of Education Committees, had to go to press with knowledge of the defeat, but prior to the confidence vote. It too took a dim view of the antics in the House. The amendment, it argued, was on 'an economic and not an educational issue and everyone connected with education in this country will note with concern that Mr R. A. Butler is reported to have tendered his resignation to the Prime Minister. It is to be hoped there will be no question of a change of leader during the passage of this Bill' (*Education*, 31 March 1944, p. 383). A week later, Sir Percival Sharp, writing in the same journal, condemned the rebels more forthrightly:

> 'Please, m'm, it came to pieces in my hand': the agitated plea of the careless parlour maid with broken china. This appears to have been the somewhat rueful attitude of, at least, some of those responsible for the defeat of the government, gazing ruefully as they did on this mischief of their handiwork.
>
> (*Education*, 7 April 1944, p. 409)

In his editorial in the *TES*, Harold Dent expressed similar sentiments:

> The progress of the Bill received an unwelcome check this week. . . .
> The division was no isolated or fortuitous incident; it was the
> culmination of a growing feeling of frustration among some
> backbenchers.
>
> But, [Dent continued] when all allowance has been made for the
> reasons which prompted the supporters of Mrs Keir's amendment to
> press it to a division, their action was ill-judged and unfair . . .
> involving a Minister who, with his measure, had every right to
> greater consideration.
>
> (*TES*, 1 April 1944)

In any case, Dent pointed out, Butler's decision had since been vindicated as leaders of both local authorities and teacher unions had assured him of their support.

With hindsight, the cause which Cazalet Keir and Hogg promoted seems so clearly just that it is easy to sympathize with them. Judged in the context of the time and place, their act was frivolous, naïve and dangerous, threatening as it did the most important domestic reform passed during the war. As we have seen, the leading advocates of reform within education swung rapidly behind Butler.

Once the moment of drama was past, it rapidly became evident that the result of the fiasco was to assist Butler. Percival Sharp realized this soon afterwards:

> The unhappy incident may affect the texture of proceedings in the
> remaining stages of the Bill. Members on the one hand may be less
> disposed to press their views to extremes. The Minister, Mr Butler,
> on the other hand, may be more disposed to such concessions as he
> can make.
>
> (*Education*, 7 April 1944, p. 409)

So it proved. The whole question of education reform and local government, which arose only after the equal pay amendment and had been widely anticipated to be difficult, provoked little controversy. Butler remembered the benefit to himself of the whole affair:

> the equal pay fracas paid a handsome dividend. . . . This made it
> very much easier to deal with the potentially controversial abolition
> of the Part III authorities.
>
> (Butler, 1971, p. 122)

THE BILL IN THE COMMONS: 3

By 8 April the *TES* editorial was celebrating the conclusion of the committee stage. Sixteen Parliamentary days had been used and there had been no resort to the guillotine; only the voluntary timetable which Butler had agreed in early March with the leading protagonists. What the *TES* found most remarkable was that 'there was an almost complete absence of the spirit of acrimony which has been so consistent a feature of educational law-making in the past'. After praising both Butler and Ede, the editorial predicted that 'it may be safely said that the form of the Act is now assured'. The task for the education service was how to achieve 'the furnishing of the framework' which the Act provided (*TES*, 8 April 1944).

A week later, the NUT, then overwhelmingly the largest teacher union, held its annual conference at Central Hall, Westminster. G. C. T. Giles, the incoming president, said that with all its limitations the Bill was a great step forward to a democratic system of education. Union members, he claimed euphorically, would cease to complain about extraneous duties. There was nothing they would not undertake to achieve that 'happier childhood and that better start in life' which was the aim of the Bill (quoted in *TES*, 15 April 1944).

From the perspective of the 1990s, after a series of Acts which can hardly be said to have mobilized the enthusiasm of the teaching profession, the vibrant optimism of Giles's speech seems remarkable and refreshing. The conference itself passed a motion which began:

> Conference extends a warm welcome to the Education Bill now before Parliament as a step towards equality of opportunity within a democratic system of education. . . . Conference pledges the full co-operation of the Union in the task of giving effect to the provisions of the Bill.
>
> (reported *ibid.*)

From Easter 1944 on, the Bill enjoyed a smooth passage through to Royal Assent.

The report stage, on 9 May, resulted in a significant number of further amendments, but not in any major change of policy direction. A number of them were moved to meet the views that had been expressed during the committee stage. The first one, moved by Butler, was to rename the President of the Board of Education, Minister of Education. He concluded his brief speech by saying, 'I trust a rose by any other name will smell as sweet' (Hansard, 9 May 1944).

Most of the other amendments were technical in nature. One exception to the rule was Lieutenant-Colonel Sir Thomas Moore, MP for Ayr Burghs, who moved that there should be included in the section on adult education, 'part time education for all male persons in the duties and obligations of citizenship and in the elementary functions of the Armed Forces of the Crown', and 'part time education for all female persons in homecraft, motherhood and the responsibilities of citizenship'. His amendment reflected strongly held views among some backbench Conservative MPs; it posed little threat to Butler, however, since to introduce such a major new element of policy at the report stage was frowned upon.

Lt.-Col. Moore acknowledged this by apologizing at the outset. He soon became further embarrassed because Rear-Admiral Beamish who had planned to support him failed to turn up.

> The future of our country depends upon whether our youth accepts its full responsibility towards its neighbour, its family and the state. The Armed Forces . . . are a means . . . of teaching adolescents self-discipline, reliability and honesty. . . . As regards our girls, I think every father and mother would admit that they and their children would have been very much better had they been taught homecraft and motherhood.
>
> (Hansard, 9 May 1944)

At this point, much of the House dissolved into laughter. It was the nearest the debates on the Bill came to sexual innuendo.

Butler intervened, hoping to minimize the embarrassment of his lobby fodder: 'Does my hon. and gallant friend mean mothercraft?' But Lt.-Col. Moore meant 'mothercraft and motherhood', he asserted: 'I am certain that the future of our race, mixed though it be, would be far sounder' if local authorities were required to ensure that these subjects were taught.

Moore found little support. The MP for Liverpool (Scotland Division), Mr Logan, felt that 'It would be better to keep girls off the streets at night, to have a curfew for them and for their mothers and fathers as well, so that they would all be in their homes at a proper time each night.'

W. G. Cove, the sharp and witty Labour MP, and spokesperson for the NUT, took a more serious view of Moore's proposals: 'In his tone and attitude, and in some of the expressions he used, I thought he was very near Hitler.'

In wartime this was brutal and direct. In any case, Cove went on, the better aspects of what Moore was suggesting, such as citizenship, were already being taught. School promoted citizenship better than any other social institution: 'If the sense of citizenship is destroyed it is destroyed on the streets, it is destroyed in slumdom, it is destroyed in bad housing, it is destroyed, I believe, in the cinemas.'

Butler summed up sympathetically but firmly. What he said of citizenship summarized his views generally on the curriculum: 'If we tried to impose the ideas of the Minister for Education, we should never get agreement on the floor of the House.'

Two days later, the report stage was concluded and Chuter Ede moved immediately that 'the Bill be read the third time'. The debate on the third reading (11 May 1944) was largely congratulatory. Apart from a brief parting whinge from a Roman Catholic MP who had played no part in the committee debates, all was sweetness and light. Sir Geoffrey Shakespeare was typical:

> I welcome the opportunity of adding my modest spray to the large bouquet which the Minister has now collected – and deservedly so – from all sides of the House . . . ever since 1921 when I became associated with this House, I have never seen a Bill that was so full of controversy, or potential controversy, more skilfully piloted through its various stages.
>
> (Hansard, 11 May 1944)

The most effective word of caution came from Arthur Colegate, MP for the Wrekin, who expressed concern about technical education and argued that

> The Bill is rather like an architect's plan of a building. It is not a building; it is only a plan, and to erect a building according to that plan will be a very heavy task indeed, far heavier than many people realise. I do not mean only the work that has to be done by my Rt. Hon. Friend and his department. . . . The public and local education authorities have to play their part and it is up to everyone who is keen on seeing this Bill carried out . . . to try to make this Bill a success.

Haden Guest, MP for Islington North, made a similar point:

> I will confine my congratulations to saying that I think the Minister
> designate and the Parliamentary Secretary have done a good Parlia-
> mentary job. I reserve further congratulations for a year's time, until
> we see what they do with the great powers and the great oppor-
> tunities which this Bill will give them.

The privilege of summing up for the opposition was given to
W. G. Cove. He remarked – broadly accurately – that

> it is not true that this Bill has taken a very long time. If the history
> of past Bills of this magnitude is examined I think it will be found
> that this Bill has had a record passage to the Statute Book.

The Bill, he said, 'provides the answer to the secularism of the
century' by requiring a collective act of worship and an agreed religious education syllabus. 'The amazing thing is that that has been
accepted in all quarters and by all parties.' He then reassured the
Catholic lobby that, as he saw it, the Bill guaranteed the future of
the denominational school and then – in a typical switch – turned
to urge the Minister to demand 'efficiency' and decent 'physical
amenities' in church schools.

As regards the centralizing tendency in the Bill, he agreed
with Butler and argued that it was 'a happy combination of the
British way of authoritarianism and libertarianism'. He certainly
welcomed the curricular freedom the schools had. He concluded
by arguing for smaller class sizes and for recognition of the
importance of education in the post-war world if Britain was to
succeed.

Butler rose to conclude the debate. The sense of achievement he
felt gushes from the pages of *Hansard* even now. He recalled that
he had intended to start in 1941 by making a few speeches up and
down the country but that an official had asked acerbically: 'Do
you realise there is only one speech to make on education? Once
you have made that, there will be nothing more for you to do.' He
had therefore decided to spend 'laborious days' preparing to settle
the disputes which for so long had plagued education reform. Wartime, 'which might seem, at first sight, the most unsuitable . . . in
practice, proved the most suitable'.

He then explained the success of his team in a way which

latter-day policy-makers might well consider worth thinking about.

> I think one reason [for our success] has been that we have had ample opportunity to try out this reform on the road, before we brought it here to be properly examined.
>
> When I say that I want to confess that we have made a great many mistakes together, which hon. members have not been able to see because we have made them in other places. When we came here, we were really proficient at our art. . . . Another reason . . . is that we decided at the outset to make the reform as comprehensive as possible, and if there were any nettles, to get a good bunch of them in our arms and not be stung just by a little one. That policy has proved extremely successful . . . because the more nettles you collect, the more they sting each other and the less they sting you. That policy appears to be a valuable one, which I shall always bear in mind if I have to tackle similar problems in the future.
>
> (Hansard, 12 May 1944)

His speech from then on consisted of reassuring discussion of the key issues raised in the months of debate along with flattering references to many of the participants. He concluded with a typically balanced piece of Butler rhetoric:

> We understand that there is a spirit in which we can all work together. We understand that there are many issues for the country still to decide, spiritual issues, social issues and economic issues. But the great thing we can feel in passing this Bill is that the structure we have here does violence to no one's conscience, it gives opportunity to everyone's individuality and upon that structure there can be built a system of education which will make the world a better place, and life a worthier thing.

The Hansard concludes formally:

> Question put, and agreed to. Bill accordingly read the Third time and passed.

The Bill's passage through the House of Commons had taken 19 days as opposed to an astonishing 59 days for the 1902 Education Act. The 1993 Education Act, which is almost twice as long as the 1944 Act and was amended over 1,000 times during its passage, was debated for just 21 days in the House of Commons.

Recording Butler's success, the *TES* was in celebratory mood:

> The creation and the successful pilotage of this Bill so far constitute
> a remarkable and . . . unprecedented achievement. . . . Pray that
> the nation will not falter when it comes to the operation of the Act.
>
> (*TES*, 20 May 1944, p. 241)

By then too, the education service was celebrating the publication
of the careful and coherent views of the McNair Committee on the
supply, recruitment and training of teachers. It had recommended
a significant increase – 15,000 per annum – in the annual supply of
teachers in order to ensure the 250,000 teachers needed for primary
and secondary schools. It called for significant salary increases to
attract able people into teaching and proposed to replace the
invidious distinctions between groups of teachers with a single cate-
gory of 'qualified teacher'. This title could only be earned by some-
one who was well educated, professionally trained and who had
successfully completed a period of probation. Universities, training
colleges and schools should be knitted together in partnership. Like
the Burnham settlement that followed the 1944 Act, and aspects
of the Act itself, McNair's report was a victory above all for the
NUT, whose influence was rarely, if ever, greater than in the
mid-1940s.

In terms of the passage of the Act, the McNair Report was
critical because it provided sober answers to the questions many
MPs and peers had asked consistently about the provision of
teachers once the war was over. During the final stages of the
Bill's passage through the Commons, Butler had demonstrated his
acceptance of the report by amending the Bill to enable boys and
girls in senior and technical schools to qualify for training as
teachers. There was surprise and delight from all commentators.
Butler's successful political use of the major reports during his
period in office was never better exemplified than in this practical
gesture.

THE BILL IN THE LORDS

The Bill began its passage through the Lords with a three-day
second reading debate in the Lords in the first full week in June.
Overall, the debates were of far less significance than those in the
Commons. One major reason for this was that most of the potentially divisive issues had either been squared by Butler and Ede

prior to the introduction of the Bill, or debated decisively in the Commons. Such was the consensus created by the end of the Commons stage that the Lords were in no position to challenge it, even had they wanted to.

Also detracting from the Lords debate were the momentous events taking place away from Parliament. Even the *TES* strayed from education altogether for its first news item of that week. It is worth quoting in full. 'Home Front' was the headline.

> Everyone's thoughts this week are with the men on the invasion fronts. It is difficult to concentrate on any work which does not seem immediately concerned with the physical battle for the liberation of the world from Nazi tyranny. The teacher's task at present must be particularly exacting, for in addition to personal emotions, there are those of excited classes to control and direct; and the routine of the schoolroom must at moments seem intolerably remote from the great and stirring actions now in hand. It is, in fact, intimately related to them. Our sailors, soldiers and airmen are today laying the foundations for victory, peace and freedom. To build securely on those foundations will be largely the task of the children now in the schools. It is in their hearts and minds that ultimate victory will be found.
>
> (10 June 1944, p. 277)

Given the overwhelming focus on the Normandy landings, which began on the same day as the second reading debate, it is hardly surprising that, as the *TES* that week pointed out, no new points of substance were raised, though the McNair Report enabled the issue of teacher supply and training to be given a more thorough airing.

The Bishop of Chichester, one of the most sceptical Anglicans, complained that the Bill would produce no lasting settlement. The Earl of Perth carped that the Bill did not do justice to Roman Catholic parents and children, but the overwhelming majority of speakers were positive, and Lord Selbourne found summing up straightforward. The Bill was read a second time without the need for a division (*TES*, 10 June 1944).

It was two weeks before the Bill went into committee. There was only one accident in the intervening period, but it had no impact on the Bill. On 17 June the *TES* reported, under the headline 'Mr Butler's Mishap':

> His many friends – and he has very many in the world of education – were sorry to learn of the President's mishap last Sunday

when he fell and fractured some ribs. . . . Latest reports state that
he is making satisfactory progress.

The committee stage, which began on 20 June, would have done
nothing to prolong Butler's period of incapacity. As the *TES* put
it on the 24th, 'No material changes were made to the Bill.' Their
Lordships ploughed politely through a series of largely technical
amendments. An attempt, similar to the one in the Commons, to
require the curriculum to include 'teaching as to the right and duty
of the citizen to defend his native land' (Hansard, 21 June 1944)
was rebuffed easily, though Lord Selbourne, for the government,
blundered by suggesting that Butler would issue regulations on the
theme. He corrected this at the report stage when the issue was
raised again.

The only defeat of any significance the government suffered in
the committee stage came on 27 June when Earl Stanhope, a
former President of the Board of Education, moved that the name
'County Colleges' be substituted for 'Young People's Colleges'. The
Earl of Selbourne, for the government, opposed the proposal,
arguing that the young people's colleges should take the name of
the town in which they were situated. In any case, it would be a
disadvantage to change a label which had been used in countless
meetings up and down the country. Viscount Cranborne, the
Leader of the House of Lords, supported Selbourne, but their suggestion that the matter be left to the report stage was not acceptable
to Stanhope, whose amendment was agreed without a division
(*TES*, 1 July 1944).

The report stage in mid-July was not quite plain sailing for the
government. As the *TES* explained:

> The Lords have not been altogether helpful over the Report Stage
> of the Education Bill. On Tuesday [11 July] they accepted, against
> the wishes of the government, an amendment which deprives the
> Minister of Education of the right to freely choose the members of
> his Central Advisory Councils by requiring in respect of one-third
> of them he shall consult beforehand the President of the Board of
> Trade and the Minister of Agriculture.
>
> (*TES*, 15 July 1944)

This amendment was carried by the narrowest majority – 21
to 20 – in spite of Lord Selbourne's plea that the Minister of
Education was as keen as anyone on the subject of technical
education.

In the scale of things, this was a minor ruffle. An amendment proposed by Lord Aberdare on behalf of Lord Gorell benefited thousands of young children in the post-war era. It required transport to be made available for children under 8 who lived more than two miles (rather than three) from their school. For children over 8, three miles was considered a reasonable distance to walk.

An interesting proposal from Viscount Maugham was that LEAs should be empowered to make grants available so that children of exceptional ability and character might be able to undertake postgraduate studies. Selbourne sympathized but opposed the idea on the grounds that it raised the question of whether this was a 'proper' area for LEA expenditure. The Bishop of London thought it raised a difficult problem of selection, and the amendment was defeated (*TES*, 15 July 1944).

In spite of the occasional hiccups, the Bill completed its report stage in the Lords on Wednesday 12 July, in much the same form as it had left the Commons two months earlier.

On 27 July it concluded its Parliamentary passage when the Commons examined the amendments made by the Lords. Butler firmly rejected the suggestion that he or his successor should be required to consult the President of the Board of Trade or the Minister of Agriculture about the membership of the central advisory councils. Why, he argued, if that principle were accepted should it only be those two and not, say, the Home Secretary? On the other hand, he was at pains to stress the government's commitment to technical education: without this commitment the Bill would not succeed. The House of Commons supported him. Otherwise, they accepted the Lords' amendments, including changing the name 'Young People's Colleges' to 'County Colleges'. Butler remarked, characteristically, that it was the spirit which animated the colleges that mattered, not the name. The Parliamentary stages of the Bill were over (*TES*, 30 July 1944).

With the impeccable timing which characterized Butler's work on the Bill, the Fleming Report, on the relationship of the independent schools to the state system, had been published the day before. Though the report urged much closer collaboration between independent schools and others, it left the initiative largely with them. It provoked a worthy and wide-ranging debate, but came to little, not surprisingly since, as far as Butler was concerned, the committee had done its job by not reporting until the Bill was safely through Parliament.

On Thursday 3 August, eight months after the Bill had been published, and just over three years after Butler had been appointed President of the Board of Education, the Bill received the Royal Assent. In educational terms, a new world had begun.

Chapter 5

After

[Churchill] began aggressively by claiming that the cat did more for the war effort that I did.

R. A. Butler, *The Art of the Possible*

BUTLER'S ACT?

On 4 August 1944 Sir Percival Sharp, Secretary of the Association of Education Committees, began his weekly piece in *Education* magazine thus:

> In a short time the seal of authoritative approval will be given to Mr Butler's Bill. In these days it is given to few Ministers of State, at so early an age, to fashion and give life to an Act of such importance and social significance. To few young statesmen is given that friendly tact, that absence of overt demonstration of force and power, which have marked the passage of a Bill – loaded with possibilities of friction and even violent contention.
>
> Parliament has justly sung the praises of great men: the Minister and his able Parliamentary Secretary [Chuter Ede]: we join in the praise.
>
> (p. 129)

The editorial of the *Times Educational Supplement* the following day agreed:

> Our first, and most welcome, duty is to offer to Mr R. A. Butler the sincerest congratulations on the completion of a noble enterprise.
>
> (p. 378)

At the time then, understandably, the unanimous answer to the question, 'Whose Act was it?' was 'Butler's'.

This too was the view of historians for the first post-war generation. Authors such as Nigel Middleton, not to mention Butler himself in his autobiography, promoted the idea of it being 'Butler's Act'. More recently, however, received wisdom had been challenged implicitly perhaps by Peter Gosden in *Education in the Second World War* and explicitly by R. G. Wallace (1981). In this section of the final chapter, the competing arguments will be examined and a judgement reached on the basis not only of the evidence, but also of political analysis.

R. G. Wallace's article, 'The origins and authorship of the 1944 Education Act' remains the most cogent and well-argued academic assault on the idea that the Act was Butler's. Wallace contends that:

> Butler exerted little influence on the education aspects of the Act. It is not his Act in the sense that it embodies his policies or was designed by him. . . . He was rather the protector of other men's plans.

The principal authors, he argues, were the group of civil servants who met at the Branksome Dene Hotel in Bournemouth in late 1940 and early 1941. He shows the importance of Maurice Holmes and his colleagues who – in the preparation of the Green Book – set out the broad agenda enacted in 1944. He then examines Butler's own contribution to policy and argues that it was minimal. Butler's concern about the allocation of pupils to different types of school at 11 led to no alteration of policy; he conceded too on the issue of direct-grant schools. In short, Wallace argues, his contribution was no more than 'political and diplomatic'. Even this he qualifies, arguing that with Churchill's backing the passage of the Act through Parliament was assured.

Nevertheless, Wallace recognizes that Butler was important in ensuring that there was an Act at all. He acknowledges Butler's role in persuading Churchill to allow the Bill to proceed, though he suggests that 'After Pearl Harbor, Churchill's hostility to legislation gradually changed to indifference' (Wallace, 1981, p. 289).

He also accepts that Butler's compromise on the Dual System was an important contribution to the passage of the Act. In spite of this, he claims Butler was not 'the father of the 1944 Act'. Instead, 'his role was . . . that of midwife, and his triumph was to deliver the infant safely after a prolonged and difficult birth' (*ibid.*, p. 290). With regard to policy, Butler had been managed by the civil servants.

> Confronted with bureaucratic authority, the open-minded Butler, let alone the more radical voices of the time, made little impact. At the Board of Education in the early 1940s, the balance of power was strongly in favour of the officials and against the politicians.
>
> (*ibid.*)

Wallace's argument clearly has considerable strength. There is no doubt that the Board of Education officials were important and that much of the policy contained in the 1944 Act was already established in the Green Book while Butler was still at the Foreign Office. In judging Butler's contribution, these points need to be taken into account. Even so, Wallace's case is incomplete in two respects. Firstly, he ignores the impact of the hugely influential popular campaign. Unless this is taken into account, it is impossible to explain for a start why board officials, who in 1938 rejected every single significant recommendation of the Spens Report, decided in the winter of 1940–41 to publish proposals on education reform. Nor is it possible to explain why both the officials and Butler went to such lengths to promote legislative reform in wartime. In short, the passage of the 1944 Act owes a great deal to thousands of nameless men and women up and down the country, and to their leaders: people like Ronald Gould, Fred Clarke, Leah Manning, Archbishop Temple and so on.

Secondly, Wallace's account underestimates Butler's consideration of policy. We have seen how, on the Dual System, the issue of Part III authorities, and other areas, Butler's political compromises involved policy shifts. Surely we can surmise that on the major issues of education policy he did not swallow, unthinkingly, an official's line. Rather he gave the issues serious thought and reached the conclusion that the decisions of officials were both educationally sound and widely supported. In other words, he made a decision not to tamper with them. Doing nothing about something can be a political achievement in itself. Indeed, from the perspective of 1994, after six years of legislative hyperactivity, one could argue that the politics of doing nothing ought to be given greater recognition.

Wallace's view did not stand unchallenged for long. Kevin Jeffereys subjected it to careful scrutiny in 1984 (Jeffereys, 1984). Drawing on the Chuter Ede Diary as well as other sources, Jeffereys argues that from his appointment in 1941, Butler realized the difficulties of pursuing education reform during wartime. Indeed,

Butler took the view that his predecessor, Herwald Ramsbotham, had been removed by Churchill because of a number of high-profile speeches he had made advocating the kinds of change outlined in the Green Book. According to Chuter Ede, Butler had heard 'whispers of displeasure at Ramsbotham's advanced ideas' (Ede Diary, 21 July and 8 August). While Butler was no less committed to reform than Ramsbotham, he was far more astute politically. He knew there was no point appearing to challenge Churchill. He also knew that if the Conservative party was to be a serious political force after the war, it would have to embrace social reform. Already in 1940 he had become Chairman of the Conservative Party Committee on Post-War Reconstruction. From the outset, he understood the potential for education reform and talked to Ede about the importance of politicians rather than officials running government departments (Ede Diary, 22 July 1941).

He then ran, according to Jefferys, a two-track strategy: on the one hand settling the contentious issues, and on the other working internally to shape the thinking within government. And, Jefferys argues, important policy issues remained to be decided, not least the future of the Dual System. Butler had, as we have seen, an important political and policy role in respect of an issue on which the civil servants had lost patience. Holmes, for example, had written a memorandum on it in February 1942 arguing that 'the only sensible solution of the problem of the Dual System is to end it' (quoted in Jefferys, 1984, p. 420). This, Butler knew, was a non-runner politically. He had colleagues like Lord Selbourne, the Minister for Economic Warfare, who considered Blackmoor School 'to be my own private property and I certainly would not give it up' for the scheme outlined in the White Paper. Butler described him to Ede as 'a bonehead', but knew that if he was to have a Bill he needed ingenuity in policy solutions as well as presentational skills. He demonstrated both during 1942 and 1943.

Jefferys contends that this contribution was immensely significant. He also points to other new policy: he cites Butler's work on the replacement of the Board of Education by a new Ministry of Education and the establishment of the central advisory councils. Jefferys further advocates greater recognition of Chuter Ede's role, particularly in relation to the local government role in education. If giving due recognition to Ede does not enhance Butler's role, it clearly does nothing to strengthen the case of those who see the civil servants as the driving force.

Overall, it would seem that while Wallace performed an important historiographic service by emphasizing the role of the civil servants at the Board, Jeffereys provides the more balanced picture. Both agree that Butler's political contribution was immense. As Jeffereys argues, he had three broad political tasks: to win governmental approval for legislating at all; to build a programme which could find support on both sides of the House of Commons; and to convince Churchill of the value of the reform.

Butler achieved the first of these tasks masterfully. He worked steadily to win the support of the Lord President's Committee. On the whole, Labour ministers were supportive. They were ever-anxious lest the deceit of 1918, when comprehensive social reform was promised but not delivered, would occur again. Some practical measure of progress during the war itself appealed. Ernest Bevin, the former Transport and General Workers' Union General Secretary, and in the war the most formidable of Labour politicians, was an avid supporter of Butler's efforts. As Ede noted in his diary, in the Lord President's Committee, Bevin could be relied on to give the Conservative ministers 'a good kick up the pants' (Ede Diary, 21 October 1942).

The leading Conservative politicians were a much tougher proposition for Butler. Cautious by political temperament about radical reform, and fearful of committing public expenditure except directly on the war effort, they took some convincing. Butler's understanding of the Conservative mind and his shrewd political judgement enabled him to coax them into supporting him over a period of time.

He exploited the strength of his own reform proposals relative to those of other ministers. The proposals in housing, agriculture and health were at an early stage of development compared to those in education. For this he owed a debt to the Board of Education officials for their foresight. The chief rival for attention was the social security plans put forward in the Beveridge Report of December 1942. It is hard to imagine the overwhelming interest in Beveridge's report. The wily old Liberal was an avid self-publicist and his theme was one of the utmost importance to people brought up in the 1930s (that 'low, dishonest decade', as Auden called it), and radicalized by the national unity of wartime. A huge queue over a mile long built up in Kingsway on the day of the report's publication. Within months it had sold 800,000 copies. The government and Churchill in particular felt threatened, unable and unwilling to promise the blank cheque they felt Beveridge's report required and antipathetic to the man's devious and publicity-conscious approach, which they abhorred. In short, Beveridge's game plan of forcing the government into action through overwhelming public pressure backfired. He had overplayed his hand.

Butler, by contrast, had moved with caution, ensuring by turns that he had solutions to controversial problems and that his cabinet colleagues knew what he was doing. In a note to Holmes and Wood on 6 July 1942 he wrote, 'my only competition appears to be Sir William Beveridge whose shield is fortunately tarnished by grimy coal and oil stains' (6 July 1942, quoted in Jeffereys, 1984). A year later, reflecting on the wave of publicity Beveridge had whipped up, he commented that his report had been

> bruited abroad. . . . The result has been that the Beveridge Plan has not marched hand in hand with that gentlemanly instinct which is so vital a feature of the Conservative Party and without which the Conservative Party cannot be brought to undertake any reform. There is a feeling about that Beveridge is a sinister old man, who wishes to give away a great deal of other people's money.
> (9 September 1943, Butler Papers, quoted in Jeffereys, 1984, p. 426)

With hindsight it is easy to see how good Butler's judgement was. In early 1943 it must have required considerable nerve and courage to keep the steady, low-key approach when Beveridge featured in the headlines and the government was consistently being accused of vacillation on education.

With his colleagues, Butler also scored over Beveridge because his plans were carefully costed and a great deal cheaper. As Kingsley Wood remarked to him in September 1942, he would rather put money into Butler's education plans than 'throw it down the sink with Sir William Beveridge' (quoted in Jeffereys, 1984, p. 426). His Conservative cabinet colleagues were increasingly able to understand the need for their party to support some social reform. 'They have been prompted to come the way of education,' wrote Butler, 'because it has been very difficult to obtain agreement between the [political] parties on any matters which involve property and the pocket' (Butler, 9 September 1943, Butler Papers, quoted in Jeffereys, 1984, p. 426).

Butler's success in gaining the support of the leading members of his own party was decisive in swinging the Parliamentary Conservative party behind him. As we have seen, he had little respect for most of them. They had little to do during wartime, a fact which made Butler even more anxious. As he said, they 'spent most of the time in the Smoking Room consuming expensive drinks and intriguing among themselves'. They were, in any case, as Alderman Byng Kenrick had warned him, abysmally ignorant about education (Ede Diary, 8 April 1942, quoted in Jeffereys, 1984, p. 426). Butler prepared them gently; at the crucial moment in the autumn of 1943, just before the Bill was introduced, he spent time with them individually. By then he was sure of the support both of Conservative leaders and the Church of England. For the average Tory backbencher in 1943, that was enough.

The Catholic elements in the party, led by the Cecil clan, remained hostile but isolated. On the Labour side the only voice of doubt came from Morrison, who wanted to see the Beveridge proposals prioritized. Since this was politically impossible, he was in no position to cause any great difficulties for Butler.

The balance of the Bill when it was published was perfectly struck – radical and coherent enough to ensure enthusiastic support from Labour, while being tactful and moderate in settling or avoiding those issues most likely to upset the Conservatives. In this sense it was very much Butler's Bill. The fact that it was being debated at all was also a personal triumph for Butler. A lesser politician would have given up hope of achieving reform the moment the Prime Minister rebuffed the idea. This Churchill did within months of Butler's appointment:

> It would be the greatest mistake to raise the 1902 controversy during the war and I certainly cannot contemplate a new Education Bill. . . . We cannot have any party politics in wartime and both your second and third points [the Dual System and the public schools] raise these in a most acute and dangerous form. Meanwhile, you have a good scope as an administrator.
>
> (Churchill to Butler, 13 September 1941,
> quoted in Howard, 1987, p. 115)

From that moment on, Butler was playing the long game. He

was greatly encouraged by support from Labour politicians; Ede certainly, but also Attlee and Bevin. Clearly he feared, well into 1942, that Churchill would block his plans or that Lords Cherwell and Beaverbrook – Churchill's 'sinister bodyguard', as he called them – would keep him out of the picture.

In the end, Butler's patient persuasion of Kingsley Wood and others, and the steady improvement of Britain's prospects in the war during 1942 and 1943, opened the way for him. By 1943 even Churchill was beginning to recognize the importance of post-war reconstruction, and, given his hostility to Beveridge, Butler's plans provided the best alternative.

Butler received an invitation to spend the night of 11 March 1943 at Chequers. Churchill's intentions soon became clear: he wanted to make use of Butler's talent in drafting a speech which would range widely across the home front. After a couple of games of bagatelle, dinner and a film about Tsarist Russia, Churchill gave Butler the part of his speech about education and asked him to come and see him the following morning. Butler related the events in some detail in his autobiography. He had already heard Churchill declaim the section of the speech on education before the film. Butler wrote:

> His theme was that we must adhere to our traditions, but that we must move from the class basis of our politics, economics and education to a national standard. There were some sharp words about idle people whether at the top or the bottom, some very pungent words about the old school tie (the time for which, he said, was past) and a definite assertion that the school-leaving age must be raised to 16.
>
> (Butler, 1971, p. 112)

The last promise was in there, Churchill said, because his daughter Mary claimed it had already been promised. Butler worked on the speech in the night, added a piece on religion, modified the promise on the school-leaving age, and made other changes.

> I was up before nine next morning and was rather shaken to be told that it wasn't certain whether the PM would actually want to see me. However, at a quarter to eleven, I found him in bed, smoking a Corona, with a black cat curled up on his feet. He began aggressively by claiming that the cat did more for the war effort than I did since it provided him with a hot water bottle and saved fuel and power. Didn't I agree? I said not really, but that it was a very beautiful cat.

Churchill then discussed his speech with Butler and drifted into reflections about his role after the war. Then he came to the subject of education. Butler described the crucial conversation:

> 'I advise you not to come out too much on education immediately,' he declared, 'because it will only drag you down in the present political atmosphere. . . . You will have to make a great statement when the time comes – a State Paper or a speech, a great speech.'

At this point, Butler took his courage in both hands.

> I said that I was drafting a Bill, with the aid of my colleagues. To this he paid no attention at all. I repeated, in a louder voice, 'I am drafting an Education Bill.' Without raising his head from the papers before him on the counterpane, he said simply that I must show him my plans when they were ready and that he was sure they would be very interesting. I gladly left it at that.
>
> (*ibid.*, pp. 114–15)

In short, Butler's tact and mastery of Conservative micro-politics had brought not only his party but also its all-important leader in behind his grand design. His experience of the India Bill and the backing of the Coalition Cabinet ensured that he was able to pilot it through the Parliamentary process with commendable smoothness.

As we have seen, there were many contributors to the contents of the 1944 Act, from campaigners in the country to officials at the Board. Nevertheless, the fact that there was an Act at all, its precise content in terms both of what was left in and of what was left out, and its safe passage were largely Butler's own personal achievement, though he himself acknowledged the contribution from James Chuter Ede, 'this consistently loyal and wise friend' (Butler, 1971, p. 93).

On its passage in August 1944, Butler was gratified to receive a telegram which read:

> Pray accept my congratulations. You have added a notable Act to the Statute Book and won a lasting place in the history of British Education. Winston S. Churchill.
>
> (quoted in Butler, 1971, p. 122)

Churchill's judgements are notoriously unreliable, but in this case we can agree with him. The evidence is conclusive: the landmark legislation of 1944 was Butler's Act.

THE ACT EVALUATED

One of the virtues of the reforms of the 1940s was the recognition by Butler and his colleagues that legislation alone does not make happier people or bring about improvements in the quality of education, or any other service. All legislation can do is establish a framework within which change can take place. Evaluating the influence of a piece of legislation is a difficult process, involving as it does the need to separate the consequences of the Act itself from the successes and failures of those responsible for administering education after its passage.

Taking the long view of the Act, there is no doubt that it created a framework within which the education system both expanded and, incrementally, developed. The Act provided a basic administrative framework which lasted until 1993. The idea of 'a national system locally administered' proved highly durable and adaptable. At the time, the Act was perceived as a centralizing measure. There is no doubt that it increased the power of the state in two ways. Firstly, it gave the state at local level – the LEAs – a much greater degree of control than ever before over the voluntary schools. This enabled them to plan, over a generation, for the provision of decent school buildings, the end of all-age schools, and the development of secondary education for all. The disastrous lack of investment in schools, especially voluntary schools, which had blighted education in the first half of the century was brought to an end.

Secondly, the Act gave the new Ministry of Education a great deal more influence over LEAs than its predecessor, the Board, had exercised. It was in particular its power to require LEAs to draw up plans for the reorganization of their schools that provided the impetus for progress in the immediate post-war period. In fact, once those years had passed, the Ministry failed to exercise its powers to the full, a failure which, with hindsight, can be seen to have contributed to the problems that have beset the education system since the mid-1970s.

One feature of the Act, therefore, was the balance it achieved between local and central control. There is no doubt that the wide discretion it left to LEAs not only allowed for diversity, but also motivated and encouraged them. In the aftermath of the war, the sheer enthusiasm with which LEAs went about their tasks is startling. Brian Simon quotes Martin Wilson, Chief Education

Officer in Shropshire from 1936 to 1965, reflecting on the post-war period:

> There was, of course, too much of everything to be done at once, and thus high pressure, much tension and turbulence, feverish endeavour liable to be thwarted by events. Piles of paperasserie. A multitude of meetings. A clangour of consultations and claims. No hours enough in the seven days [but] tremendously invigorating, taut, demanding, challenging, speculative, open.
>
> (quoted in Simon, 1991, p. 89)

This distribution of influence and responsibility is surely much to the Act's credit, since we know from management research what was then known intuitively: that successful reform depends on inspiring motivation at all levels.

The Act also inspired motivation because it provided for those long-cherished goals of teachers and other reformers: secondary education for all and a unified education service. 'At long last' might have summarized the feelings of many teachers. C.G.T. Giles, President of the NUT in the year the Bill became an Act, certainly saw it this way in his book *The New School Tie* (1946). Referring to Ellen Wilkinson, the first Labour Minister of Education, he wrote: '[we] share with her a tremendous task and a grand opportunity. . . . The old is dead. We shall die with it unless we can give birth to the new' (quoted in Simon, 1991, p. 96).

Also greatly to the Act's credit is the huge expansion of educational provision which took place in the post-war generation. In 1938 education expenditure was 3 per cent of gross national product; by 1961 it was 4.5 per cent. In 1947 there were just over 5 million pupils in maintained schools: by 1965 there were 9.1 million. The number of teachers increased from 175,275 in 1946 to 448,034 in 1977; the number of university students from 38,000 in 1944 to 139,000 in 1964. True, all this took time; true too that the last all-age pre-Hadow school was not reorganized until 1972; even so the extent of progress is impressive. The Act also brought about a degree of political consensus which meant that the acrimony of the 1920s and 1930s was forgotten. The debates and disputes of the 1940s and 1950s were about quality and extent rather than direction. Only in the mid-1960s did this consensus begin to break up.

If this is the case for the Act, what of the case against? Certainly in relation to its implementation there were many disappointments.

Within a few months of Labour's historic election victory in 1945 there was pressure in the Cabinet to delay the raising of the school-leaving age to 15.

Within two weeks of the Royal Assent in 1944, Butler had postponed the implementation of the new school-leaving age until a date not later than 1 April 1947. Ellen Wilkinson was able to sustain this date in the Cabinet in 1945 despite pressure from some cabinet colleagues, including Aneurin Bevan, whose chief concern was the housing programme. The issue re-emerged in January 1947, just three months before the appointed day. A cabinet committee chaired by the Chancellor of the Exchequer, Hugh Dalton, recommended a five-month delay because of its cost and its effect on the labour force. Wilkinson successfully saw off this challenge in the Cabinet shortly before her death.

Other aspects of the Act fared less well. The leaving age of 16 was not achieved until 1972. Compulsory part-time attendance at the county colleges for all 15- to 18-year-olds was never implemented at all; the failure of the early 1920s being repeated in the late 1940s.

Yet it seems unfair to lay the blame for these failures on the Act itself. The Act made them possible; it established the framework within which they could have been achieved. The blame for the failure must surely lie with the politicians, both Labour and Conservative, who failed to give education in general and these issues in particular sufficient priority. While the post-war governments, especially the 1945–51 Labour government, had to work on a mass of competing priorities with strictly limited resources, the chief reason that the 1944 Education Act was not fully implemented was simply the absence of sufficient political will. Education never had the good fortune to have a minister with, for example, Bevan's passion or Macmillan's drive, and suffered as a result. Indeed, one might speculate that the Act would have fared better during its implementation phase had it been solely identified with the Labour government. As it was, its chief protagonist, Butler, was in opposition in the crucial years of the late 1940s, and Labour was setting a new agenda based on health, housing and nationalization.

Perhaps the most severe critic of the Act is Corelli Barnett, who saw it as a prime example of the New Jerusalemism – woolly, liberal-minded progressivism, as he saw it – which he so despised. Barnett notes that Butler, in his letter to Churchill just after his appointment, identified as the *first* question facing the education service the need for industrial and technical training, and the issue of the church schools as the second (Barnett, 1986, p. 283). He then criticizes him for altering his priorities in the ensuing years by giving far more attention to the second than the first. There is some validity in the criticism. Certainly, the White Paper of 1943 was slight in its coverage of technical education, and in the debates in 1944 technical education featured hardly at all. Butler, like almost everyone else in his time, was inspired by the idea of a democratic, liberal education system for all. This is hardly surprising. The British people were, after all, engaged in an ideological as well as a military conflict with Fascism. Overall, though, surely Barnett has missed the point. Butler did not spend so much time with the churches because religion was what mattered most to him. He did so because the historical record showed him that, unless he could solve the religious issues, he would not be able to bring about reform at all. The evidence of the Ede Diary shows conclusively that Ede and Butler often found the time the religious settlement absorbed tedious and distracting, but they were shrewd enough politicians to know that it had to be done. In other words, the religious settlement was not, as Barnett imagines, an *alternative* to an education reform which would have improved technical education, it was a *precondition* of it. Indeed, having settled the religious question, the Act did provide for compulsory part-time attendance of 15- to 18-year-olds at county colleges. The failure here lay not with the Act, but with its implementation. In this respect Barnett's critique is highly pertinent. A more industrially minded culture would not have allowed the politicians to drop this part of the Act off the bottom of the list of priorities. The most that can legitimately be said in criticism of the Act is that it did little to challenge the inadequacies of the prevailing culture.

Another line of criticism has been that the Act was insufficiently radical. It left the Dual System intact; it failed to challenge the role of independent schools; and it provided for an essentially selective system of secondary education. The view is summarized by Roy Lowe: 'in essence the new order in English education which [the Act] ushered in was, as Simon concludes, "the old order in a new guise" ' (Lowe, 1992, p. 14). On this interpretation, the Act is very much a Tory Act: sufficient to buy off the radical reformers but restricted enough to maintain the interests of Tory voters.

Essentially this is a matter of opinion. Certainly the case for this interpretation has been well enough made by Roy Lowe, Brian Simon and others. There are occasions when it seems Butler himself saw it this way. Throughout, Butler's judgements were intensely political. He was at the leading edge of modernizing and reforming Conservatives, and his Act was an essential part of this process. He even described the Act as 'really codifying existing practice, which always seems to me the hallmark of good legislation' (quoted in Jeffereys, 1984, p. 430). Undoubtedly the Act helped him achieve his political goals and advance his career, though not in time for the Conservatives to win in 1945.

The problem with this interpretation is that it was not seen as so conservative a measure by commentators, particularly radical ones, at the time. As it completed its passage through the Commons it was the firebrand W. G. Cove, leader of the most radical strike in NUT history in 1919, who claimed that it was 'in some respects a revolutionary Bill' (Hansard, 12 May 1944). Most of the criticisms he uttered that day concerned his anxieties about implementation after the war.

Other radicals took a similar position. We have seen the tremendous enthusiasm for the Bill of Harold Dent, editor of the *TES*, and the leaders of the NUT at the time. The speech of C. G. T. Giles, the communist President of the NUT in 1944, has already been quoted. Ronald Gould, the President in 1943 and General Secretary from 1946, was full of praise for Butler. The leadership of the Labour Party had been among his most enthusiastic supporters throughout his period at the Board of Education. The fact is that after the intense frustrations and bitter disappointments of the 1920s and 1930s, Butler's Act was a tremendous, and radical, breakthrough. Neither he nor his Act can be held responsible for the fact that its proposals had not been implemented a generation earlier. That so radical a measure could be piloted through the Parliament of diehards elected in 1935 was a remarkable testimony not only to the huge shift in political climate wrought by the war, but also to the political insight and skill of Butler.

While he saw it as the harbinger of a new modern conservatism, most of those on the Left recognized that at the time it was as radical an Act as could be achieved. No wonder the debate about whether it was conservative or radical rumbles on, since clearly it was both. Butler was a radical Conservative and the radicals were desperate enough for change to be pragmatic.

In any case, while the debate is of academic interest, even those who choose to pigeonhole the Act as limited and conservative must acknowledge a major virtue of the Act: it was flexible. Radical or not in 1944, it provided the framework within which both the essentially conservative tripartite system flourished in the 1950s and the progressive comprehensive system developed in the late 1960s and 1970s. Such a framework is in strong contrast to the kind of rolling, detailed legislative programme which has characterized the late 1980s and early 1990s, and which has brought about the demise of Butler's Act. Overall, it might be concluded with some confidence that the 1944 Education Act provided the legislative foundation on which a successful education system might have been built through political and administrative endeavour. Whether or not the fifty years since then have been broadly successful or not is a fascinating but quite separate question. Whatever else is said about R. A. Butler, we can surely all agree that the impact of his work was, at least in the long run, a great deal more positive than that of Churchill's cat.

Bibliography

Adelman, P. (1977) *The Road to 1945*. London: Quartet.

Barber, M. (1992) *Education and the Teacher Unions*. London: Cassell.

Barnett, C. (1986) *The Audit of War*. London: Macmillan.

Batho, G. (1989) *Political Issues in Education*. London: Cassell.

Board of Education (1926) *Report of the Consultative Committee on the Education of the Adolescent* (The Hadow Report). London: HMSO.

Board of Education (1938) *Report of the Consultative Committee on Secondary Education with Special Reference to Grammar Schools and Technical High Schools* (The Spens Report). London: HMSO.

Board of Education (1941) *Education after the War* (Green Book). London: HMSO.

Board of Education (1943a) *Educational Reconstruction* (White Paper). London: HMSO.

Board of Education (1943b) *Curriculum and Examinations in Secondary School* (The Norwood Report). London: HMSO.

Board of Education (1944a) *The Public Schools and the General Educational System: Report of the Committee on Public Schools* (The Fleming Report). London: HMSO.

Board of Education (1944b) *Report of a Committee Appointed by the President of the Board of Education to Consider the Supply, Recruitment and Training of Teachers and Youth Leaders* (The McNair Report). London: HMSO.

Butler, R. A. (1971) *The Art of the Possible*. London: Hamish Hamilton.

Calder, A. (1969) *The People's War: Britain 1939–45*. London: Jonathan Cape.

Clarke, F. (1923) *Essays in the Politics of Education*. Oxford: Clarendon Press.

Clarke, F. (1943) *Education and Social Change*. London: SPCK.

Curtis, S. J. (1952) *Education in Britain since 1900*. London.

Dent, H. C. (1943) *Education in Transition*. London: University of London Press.

Ede, James Chuter, *Diary* (British Library MSS 59690–59702).

Education magazine (official organ of the Association of Education Committees), weekly 1940–45.

Gilbert, M. (1991) *Churchill: A Life*. London: Heinemann.

Giles, C. G. T. (1946) *The New School Tie*. London.

Gordon, P., Aldrich, R. and Dean, D. (1991) *Education and Policy in England in the Twentieth Century*. London: The Woburn Press.

Gosden, P. H. J. H. (1976) *Education in the Second World War: A Study in Policy and Administration*. London: Methuen.

Gosden, P. H. J. H. (1972) *The Evolution of a Profession*. Oxford: Blackwell.

Gould, Sir R. (1976) *Chalk up the Memory*. Birmingham: Alexander.

Hansard (The Official Report House of Commons, 5th Series) – citations in text give date of debate.

HMSO (1944) *The Education Act 1944*. London: HMSO.

Howard, A. (1987) *RAB: The Life of R. A. Butler*. London: Jonathan Cape.

Jeffereys, K. (1984) 'R. A. Butler, the Board of Education and the 1944 Act', *History* **69** (227).

Journal of Education, 1940–45.

Lowe, R. (ed.) (1992) *Education and the Second World War*. London: Falmer.

Lowndes, G. A. N. (1969) *The Silent Social Revolution, 1895–1965*. Oxford: Oxford University Press.

Middleton, N. and Weitzman, S. (1976) *A Place for Everyone*. London: Gollancz.

Mitchell, F. W. (1967) *Sir Fred Clarke: Master Teacher 1880–1952*. London: Longman.

Parliamentary Debates (*Hansard*): various 1943–44.

Simon, B. (1974) *The Politics of Education Reform 1920–1940*. London: Lawrence & Wishart.

Simon, B. (1991) *Education and the Social Order 1940–1990*. London: Lawrence & Wishart.

Simon, J. (1989) 'Promoting educational reform on the Home Front: The *TES* and *The Times* 1940–44', *History of Education* **18** (3).

Times Educational Supplement, weekly 1940–45.

Wallace, R. G. (1981) 'The origins and authorship of the 1944 Education Act', *History of Education* **10** (4).

Index

Aberdare, Lord 105
Adams, W. G. S. 6–7
adult education 67, 69, 73–4,
    80, 98
agricultural lobby 2
'All Souls Group' 6
Anderson, J. 38
assessment 64
Assisted Places Scheme 53
Association of Directors and
    Secretaries of Education
    11
Association of Education
    Committees 28, 42, 46,
    49–50, 69, 71–2, 95, 107
Association of Metropolitan
    Counties 49
Astor, Lady Nancy 84–5, 89
Attlee, Clement 38, 114

Baldwin, R. D. 40
Barnett, Corelli 4–5, 17, 118–19
Barrington-Ward, Robert 5–6
Barrow, R. H. 51
Bevan, Aneurin 118
Beveridge, Sir William 46
Beveridge Report 8, 111–13
Bevin, Ernest 52, 75, 111, 114
Birmingham, Archbishop of 58–9

Blackwell, Basil 7
Board of Education 2, 4, 7, 9,
    12–30, 34–6, 43, 49, 51,
    55, 58, 61, 63–4, 73, 81,
    98, 109–11
British Council of Churches 80
Burnham Committee 88–91
Butler, R. A.
    appointment as President of
        the Board of Education
        30, 34–6
    biographical details 7–8, 14, 32
    on centralization 100
    and the churches 26, 39–48,
        69–71, 76–9, 82
    on citizenship 99
    critical analyses of 107–15,
        118–21
    on direct-grant schools 76
    and the Dual System 76, 81
    and Education Bill (1943–44)
        37–8, 57, 69, 71, 73–80,
        82, 86–9
    on educational administration
        71–3, 82
    on educational reform 37,
        50–6
    on equal pay 89–90
    at the Foreign Office 33–4
    at the India Office 32
    and local government 48–50

on raising the school-leaving
age 75, 83, 86-7, 118
relationship with Winston
Churchill 31-8, 92-5
on teacher education 67
and White Paper (1943) 57-9,
62, 68

Campaign for Educational
Advance (CEA) 8, 11
Carr, E. H. 5
Catholic Church 2, 9-11, 23-4,
39-48, 57-9, 69-71, 73,
77-9, 100, 103, 113
Catholic Education Council 39
Cazalet Keir, Thelma 83-4, 87-8,
90, 94, 96
Central Advisory Councils 7, 73,
104-5, 110
central schools 15, 19
centralization 116
Channon, 'Chips' 36
Charles, R. H. 21
Chichester, Bishop of 45, 103
Christian Newsletter 7, 54
Church of England 2, 4, 9-11,
24, 39, 41-2, 44-6, 48, 71,
103, 113
church schools, *see* voluntary
schools
church-state relationship 9,
23-6, 37-48, 82-3
Churchill, Sir Winston 4, 30-5,
37-8, 92-4, 108, 110-11,
113-15
Chuter Ede, James 8, 23-4,
28, 30, 37-8, 40, 42-3,
49-50, 62, 70, 73, 79-80,
97, 102, 109-11, 115,
119
citizenship education 98-9
civil servants/Civil Service 88,
90, 111
Clarke, Sir Fred 6-7, 10-11, 40,
109
class size 1, 62, 86, 100

Cleary, William 16, 20, 22, 25,
51
Colgate, W. A. 91, 99
Committee of Senior Officials on
Post-War Reconstruction
12-16, 20
Communism/Communist Party
3, 9
comprehensive education/schools
9, 16, 19, 21, 51, 65, 80,
121
compulsory education 1-2, 28,
60, 75, 118-19
see also part-time education;
school-leaving age
Conservative government/Party
2, 3, 30-2, 34, 36, 38, 44,
46-7, 52-3, 59, 69, 75-6,
79-81, 86-92, 95, 110-13,
118-20
Co-operative Union 8
county colleges 104-5, 118-19
see also part-time education
County Councils Association 49,
52
Cove, W. G. 84-6, 99-100, 120
Cowper-Temple clause 41-2, 44,
46
Cranborne, Viscount 104
curriculum development 54-5,
74, 100, 104
Curtis, S. J. 56

Dalton, Hugh 118
day continuation schools 15, 22,
28, 52
Dearing, Sir Ron 55
Dent, H. C. 6-7, 54, 59, 69, 79,
96, 120
direct-grant schools 20, 51-2,
65, 76, 87, 108
Downey, Archbishop 47, 70-1
Dual System 9, 23-6, 30, 37-8,
41-3, 57, 62, 76, 78-81,
108-10, 113, 119
Duckworth, F. R. G. 21

Economist, The 13, 31, 72, 74
Eden, Anthony 33, 92
Education 58, 72, 93, 95, 107
Education Act (1870) 9
Education Act (1902) 9, 16,
    23–5, 27, 37, 41, 101
Education Act (1918) 2, 28, 36
Education Act (1921) 62
Education Act (1936) 2, 9, 12, 47
Education Act (1944) 107–21
Education Act (1993) 46, 101
Education Bill (1896) 27
Education Bill (1941) 40–1
Education Bill (1943–44)
    general aspects 23, 57, 113, 115
    in House of Commons
        committee stage 81–96
        first reading 73–4
        report stage 97–9
        Royal Assent 106
        second reading 74–80
        third reading 99–101
        voting 92, 94
    in House of Lords 102–6
educational administration 9,
    12–30, 42–5, 48–50, 60–8,
    71–2, 74, 77, 80, 110–11,
    116
    see also specific subjects, e.g.
        local education
        authorities
educational finance 2, 9–10,
    12–13, 19–21, 24, 45–7, 52,
    61–2, 66, 69–74, 77, 79–83,
    112, 117
educational opportunity 61–2, 86
educational reconstruction, *see*
    Committee of Senior
    Officials on Post-War
    Reconstruction; Green
    Book; White Paper,
    Educational Reconstruction
educational reform 4–11, 12–30,
    31, 37–40, 46–7, 50–6, 58,
    60–1, 73, 96, 109–10
    see also specific subjects, e.g.
        school-leaving age
Educational Theory Panel 16

elementary education/schools
    1–2, 6, 12, 15–16, 18–19,
    27, 41, 48, 51, 60, 62
    see also primary education/
        schools; specific types
        of school
eleven-plus examinations 62–3
equal pay 88–96
evacuation 3, 6, 12–13, 64, 75

Five Points 40–1
Fleming Committee/Report 49,
    53, 65, 67, 69, 105
Free Church Federal Council 46
further education 22, 67

Gallacher, William 91
Geddes Committee 2
Giles, G. C. T. 97, 117, 120
girls' education 98
Gorst, Sir John 27
Gosden, P. H. J. H. 15, 108
Gould, Sir Ronald 8, 10, 30, 54,
    95, 109–20
grammar schools 1–2, 16–18,
    20–2, 52
Green Book 7, 15, 17–19, 22–3,
    25–30, 34, 37, 40, 42,
    48–52, 65, 108–10
Greenwood, Arthur 79, 82, 87
Griffin, Mgr B. W. 78, 82
Gruffydd, Professor W. J. 84
Guardian, The 58
Guest, Dr Haden 88, 100

Hadow reorganization 2, 9–10,
    12, 18–19, 24, 39, 48, 117
Hadow Report 2, 10, 18–19, 24,
    27, 39
Halifax, Lord 36
Hannon, Patrick 79
Higher School Certificate 17

Hinsley, Cardinal A. 39, 42, 46-7, 70-1
Hogg, Quintin 86-7, 90, 94, 96
Holmes, Maurice 4, 13-14, 16-18, 21, 24-6, 29-30, 37, 42, 50, 108, 110
Howard, Anthony 36
Hughes, Moelwyn 84
Huxley, Julian 56

illiteracy 4
industry-education relationship 29, 75, 80
infant schools 64

James, Eric 7
Jeffereys, K. 31, 109-11
Jowitt, Sir William 49
junior schools 16, 62, 64

Kenrick, Byng 113
Key Stage 2 tests 62

Labour government/Party 2-4, 9, 15, 23, 30, 38, 43, 78-80, 87, 89, 91, 95, 111, 113, 117-18, 120
Lester-Smith, W. O. 7, 30
Liberal Party 4, 10, 111
Lindsay, Kenneth 7
Listener, The 34-6
local education authorities 9, 24-5, 27-8, 42-3, 45, 48-50, 52, 63-6, 68-9, 71, 116
Local Government Act (1929) 50
local government reorganization 48-50
Logan, D. G. 98
London, Bishop of 105

Lord President's Committee 70, 111
Lowe, Roy 3, 119, 120

McNair Report 29, 67, 102-3
Mander, Sir Frederick 14, 38, 95
Mangay, T. 90
Manning, Leah 109
Maugham, Viscount 105
Maxton, Jimmy 88-9
May Committee 2
Methodist Church 41
Middleton, Nigel 107
Ministry of Education 110, 116
Moore, Sir Thomas 81-2, 98
'Moot, The' 6
Morrison, Herbert 113
multilateral schools, *see* comprehensive education/ schools

National Association of Labour Teachers 9
National Union of Teachers 7, 10, 14, 29-30, 38, 42-9, 58, 81, 95, 97, 102, 117, 120
'New Jerusalemers' 4-5, 10, 14-15, 39, 79, 118
New Statesman 72
Newson, John 7
Nicholson, Harold 93
Nonconformist churches 24, 41-4, 47-8, 69, 73
Norwood Committee/Report 7, 53-6, 65
Norwood, Sir Cyril 10, 55
nursery education/schools 60, 62, 64, 75

Observer, The 72

parental responsibility 64
Parker, H. J. H. 78
part-time education 2, 15, 52, 61, 75, 78, 80, 98, 118-19
see also compulsory education; county colleges; day continuation schools
Part II authorities 27, 71
Part III authorities 26-7, 48-50, 57, 68-9, 71-3, 96, 109
Patten, John 60
Percy, Lord Eustace 13
Perth, Earl of 103
Picture Post 5
poverty 3
Priestley, J. B. 5
primary education/schools 18, 22, 42, 60, 66, 75
see also elementary education/ schools
public schools 1, 10-11, 37-8, 49, 53, 69, 78, 105, 113, 119
pupil population 1, 17, 24, 62, 117

Quakers 41

Raikes, H. V. A. M. 91
Ramsbotham, Herwald 29, 31, 34, 39, 110
religious education 40-5, 47, 54, 58-9, 66, 69, 100
see also church-state relationship; voluntary schools; specific denominations

Savage, Graham 51
scholarships 1, 2, 10
school buildings/maintenance 9, 17, 24-6, 44, 52, 71-2, 116
School Certificate 21

school closures 25
school fees 1, 20-1, 51-2, 63, 65, 76
school health service 67
school size 51
school worship 100
school-leaving age 1-2, 9, 12, 15-16, 19-20, 28, 30, 42, 52, 60-2, 73, 75-6, 78-80, 83-7, 114, 118
Scotland 46, 47-8
Second World War 2-6, 12, 33-4, 92-3, 103
secondary education/schools 2, 6-9, 12, 14, 15-23, 25-6, 28, 42, 45, 47, 50-1, 55, 60, 62, 64-6, 75, 108, 117, 119
see also specific types of school
'secondary education for all' 2, 8-9, 26, 30, 42, 51, 54, 116
Secondary Schools Examinations Council (SSEC) 55
secondary modern schools 20-2, 65
Selborne, Lord 44, 104-5, 110
Selby-Bigge, Sir Amherst 27
selection 20-1, 62-3, 105, 108, 119
senior schools, *see* elementary education/schools; secondary education/ schools
Shakespeare, Sir Geoffrey 78-9, 99
Sharp, Sir Percival 28, 42, 44, 50, 58, 69, 71-2, 95-6, 107
Simon, Brian 5, 11, 54-5, 119-20
Simon, Sir John 36
social class 1, 3, 11, 15, 114
social reform 4-5, 8, 20, 38-9, 46, 111-12
Southby, Sir A. 91
Spectator 7
Spens Report 2, 10-11, 12, 18-20, 27, 109

Summerskill, Edith 91
Sunday Times, The 72
surplus places 25

Tawney, R. H. 8
teacher appointment/recruitment/
supply 25, 29, 42–4, 46–8,
66–7, 78, 80, 102–3, 117
teacher education 29, 41, 67, 88,
102–3
teacher salaries 2, 9, 88–9, 102
see also Burnham Committee;
equal pay
technical education/schools
16–18, 20, 22, 51, 65, 73,
80, 99, 104–5, 119
Temple, William 5, 10, 39, 44–5,
80, 109
Thomas, Ivor 90
Thorneycroft, Peter 87–8
Times, The 4–6, 40, 58, 72,
80
Times Educational Supplement
6–8, 13, 54–8, 74, 81–2,
87, 96–7, 101–3, 107,
120
Trades Union Congress (TUC) 7,
9, 59
transfer age/policy 16, 22, 51,
62–3, 65
tripartite system 51, 54–6, 63,
65, 121

Vickers, Geoffrey 54
voluntary schools 9–10, 16, 24,
41–2, 44–7, 66, 69, 76–7,
100, 116, 119

walking distance from school 105
Wallace, R. G. 108–9, 111
Wallis, H. B. 16–17, 21
Welsh Department 16
Wheldon, Wynn 25
White Memorandum (1942) 43–5
White Paper, *Choice and
Diversity* (1992) 60–1
White Paper, *Educational
Reconstruction* (1943) 7,
50, 56–71, 73, 110, 119
Wilkinson, Ellen 117–18
Williams, G. G. 16, 20–1, 55
Williams, Sir Herbert 84–6
Williams, Shirley 76
Wilson, Martin 116–17
women's employment 3
Wood, Kingsley 38, 46, 112, 114
Wood, R. S. 13, 15–16, 20, 24, 51
Wood, S. H. 21, 24
Workers' Educational Association
(WEA) 7, 11, 81
Worsley, T. C. 11

youth service 28–9, 67, 69